Gertrude Stein

Titles in the series Critical Lives present the work of leading cultural figures of the modern period. Each book explores the life of the artist, writer, philosopher or architect in question and relates it to their major works.

Jean Genet
Stephen Barber

Michel Foucault
David Macey

Pablo Picasso
Mary Ann Caws

Franz Kafka
Sander L. Gilman

Guy Debord
Andy Merrifield

Marcel Duchamp
Caroline Cros

James Joyce
Andrew Gibson

Frank Lloyd Wright
Robert McCarter

Jean-Paul Sartre
Andrew Leak

Noam Chomsky
Wolfgang B. Sperlich

Jorge Luis Borges
Jason Wilson

Erik Satie
Mary E. Davis

Georges Bataille
Stuart Kendall

Ludwig Wittgenstein
Edward Kanterian

Octavio Paz
Nick Caistor

Walter Benjamin
Esther Leslie

Charles Baudelaire
Rosemary Lloyd

Jean Cocteau
James S. Williams

Sergei Eisenstein
Mike O'Mahony

Salvador Dalí
Mary Ann Caws

Simone de Beauvoir
Ursula Tidd

Edgar Allan Poe
Kevin J. Hayes

Gertrude Stein

Lucy Daniel

REAKTION BOOKS

Published by Reaktion Books Ltd
33 Great Sutton Street
London EC1V 0DX, UK
www.reaktionbooks.co.uk

First published 2009

Printed and bound in Great Britain
by CPI Antony Rowe, Chippenham, Wiltshire

British Library Cataloguing in Publication Data
Daniel, Lucy Jane.
    Gertrude Stein. – (Critical lives)
    1. Stein, Gertrude, 1874–1946 – Criticism and interpretation.
    I. Title   II. Series
    818.5'209-DC22

ISBN: 978 1 86189 516 5

Contents

Introduction 7

One 11

Two 24

Three 50

Four 75

Five 94

Six 117

Seven 145

Eight 173

References 195

Select Bibliography 215

Acknowledgements 221

Photo Acknowledgements 223

Writing, posed in front of her portrait, 1914, photographed by Alvin Langdon Coburn.

Introduction

The monumental presence of Gertrude Stein presides over New York's Bryant Park, serenely overlooking the New York Public Library, in the form of the sculpture by Jo Davidson first cast in Paris in 1922. Sitting in characteristic pose, pensive, relaxed, taking in the world, on the verge of laughter, she seems to represent a little bit of Montmartre transported to Midtown Manhattan. An image of Left Bank bohemia, the American in Paris has also become a Parisian in America.

What lies behind that burnished, Sphinx-like creation? The image of herself Stein projected in her work encompassed many contradictions central to modern intellectual life. Stein was a fierce patriot, and much of her work was about defining American national character, but she lived most of her life in Paris where, part-snob, part-democrat, she became the hostess of the city's most important artistic salon. She was a scientist who became a literary giant, and a serious formal experimenter who ended up a bestseller and a literary celebrity. Seen as a feminist and a lesbian icon, she was conservative in her political views; she was obsessed by middle-class values, but was also the self-appointed queen of the avant-garde.

She was perhaps the most important experimental writer of the century. Her claim to be the most *experimental* experimental writer is also closely contested. She produced, from the early 1900s onwards, work of such radical experiment that readers doubted not only her sanity but whether what she produced could even be classified as writing. In the 1930s she was reborn through a series of populist auto-hagiographies. From the beginning, the events of her life found their way wholesale into her work, while even her own works became her subject matter, and were enshrined as events in her written version, her legend, of her life.

Even before her groundbreaking autobiographies, her personality was overbearing. It was a personality and a flamboyant life story that overshadowed, and still does overshadow, her work. 'Remarks are not literature', she once told Hemingway, but much of her literary reputation was erected on the rickety foundations of her own 'remarks'. She was hoisted by her own petard by the brilliance of her self-invention. It was Edmund Wilson who wrote in 1934 that though 'her influence has always been felt at the sources of literature and art . . . neither the readers of modern books nor the collectors of modern painting have realized how much they owe her.'[1] The same is still true today. After years of solitary toiling, extraordinarily determined – almost pigheaded – adherence to her own beliefs in the theory of composition and, it is true, association with the greatness of others, Stein eventually achieved the fame she had always hungered for. This was somewhat crassly summed up in the realization of two lifelong dreams, an entry in *Who's Who* and publication in *The Atlantic Monthly* (two ambitions all the more interesting, considering the outlandishness of both her style and her personality, for being so conventional). Stein wrote a bewildering number and baffling variety of works; there are 571 separate named pieces in the Yale catalogue of her work. But, though her work spans half a century and comprises novels, poetry, portraits, stories, essays, children's books, scientific work, librettos, memoirs, plays, autobiography and lectures, as well as some work that seems genuinely unclassifiable, she remains both one of the most easily recognizable and one of the least-known of the century's great literary figures.

Her retrospective embellishments, stylizations and reiterations of momentous occasions in her own life lit up a dazzling image of the separate lives of Stein: the icon, the salonière, the patron of modern art, and the private artist, the solitary writer. 'I am writing for myself and strangers', she declared. Among the slew of memoirs of Paris in the 1920s, none is complete without at least a passing sketch of Stein and her Saturday night gatherings at the rue de Fleurus, and the real events are misted over in anecdote and vendetta. The problem for Stein's readers is often how to free her from the facade of her own making. And there is a separate story of how the cult of Gertrude Stein was created, both by herself and her constellation of admirers.

Jo Davidson, *Gertrude Stein*, 1922, bronze.

One

For anyone familiar with the bravado of Gertrude Stein's autobiographical voices, her legendary personal charisma and her stoical
declarations of her own genius, repeated like a mantra, it comes
as a shock that she chose to sum up her life, while reflecting on
Darwin's theory of evolution, as a realization of 'the fact that stars
were worlds and that space had no limitation and . . . civilizations
came to be dead . . . and I had always been afraid always would be
afraid'.[1] Death and extinction loomed over her when she thought
about her childhood: a darkness in Darwin's vision that was, she
saw, transferred to the intellectual climate of her youth, bound in
with her own adolescent melancholy, her fear of sudden death and
'dissolution'.[2] The bombast of what Djuna Barnes called her 'monstrous ego'[3] was partly a way of covering up that loneliness and fear,
as if by a series of mesmerizing, entrancing tricks she could distract
people from her insecurity. In her grandest work, *The Making of
Americans*, a book which started as a history of her own German
Jewish family and their arrival in America, this would mutate into
a megalomaniac urge to catalogue all possible variations of human
life; in her need to leave a legacy to future generations, nothing
would do other than knowing everything, and always being right.

When Gertrude was a little girl, she overheard a conversation
that would still make her shudder when she remembered it a lifetime later. Gertrude, the youngest of five siblings, was idly listening
to her parents' conversation when she gleaned the fact that another

sister had been stillborn, and another brother had died very young. Her father was adamant that he had only ever wanted five children. Had it not been for the deaths of these two babies, buried on a chilly hillside in Pennsylvania, Gertrude Stein and her beloved brother Leo would never have been born.[4] In this childhood moment of devastating realization – young Gertrude's sudden sense of herself as a cosmological fluke, clawing her way into life through the jaws of destiny – seemed to be contained, for the adult Stein, the seeds of her lifelong fascination with personality, character and identity. She would live forever with the fear of her own insignificance. And from then on, it seemed, she was also intent on creating 'a life' for herself.

At least, that's the way she told it. For this childhood memory is but one of many paradigmatic scenarios with which Stein built up her own legend, in which truth and self-invention often overlapped. Gertrude was fully aware of both the value and the artifice of presenting her life as a series of witty and eccentric tableaux. From an early age she was in pursuit of '*la gloire*'. 'Nobody really lives who has not been well written about', she declared in a memoir written near the end of her life.[5] With a Barnumesque instinct for self-promotion, she bound up anecdotes, bon mots, catchphrases and slogans into her personal myth. She even had her most famous line, 'rose is a rose is a rose is a rose', embroidered on her table-linen, printed on the china and embossed as a logo on her stationery. After the phenomenal success, in 1933, of *The Autobiography of Alice B. Toklas*, Stein's first full-length work of pure autobiography, 'God what a liar she is!' wrote her by then estranged brother, Leo.[6]

Her autobiographies cast only the occasional backwards glance that reaches as far as childhood. The state of childhood was disconcerting to the adult Stein; she wrote about the impossibility of envisioning herself as a child without irreparable damage not only to her self-image but to her image of the universe. It destroyed her sense of 'the everlasting'; it made 'a broken world'.[7] Gertrude, in fact, succeeded in being born on 3 February 1874 to Daniel and Amelia Stein in Allegheny, Pennsylvania, a town which no longer exists, having been engulfed by Pittsburgh. In many ways Stein, the arch-modernist, was a product of the nineteenth century. She envisioned herself as born into an age of science and warfare. Darwin was 'the great man of the period that framed my youth'.[8] It was selling Union uniforms during the Civil War that had turned her father's family from pedlars into wealthy manufacturers who owned a flourishing wholesale business. In her final book, Stein wrote: 'I was always in my way a Civil War veteran.'[9] Born less than a decade after the end of the Civil War, its stories surrounded her as she grew up. Her birthday was almost the centenary of the birth of the USA, and she would always proudly characterize it as the country of youth and innovation.

'It has always seemed to me a rare privilege, this, of being an American, a real American, one whose tradition it has taken scarcely sixty years to create.'[10] Stein's new America would always be defined by its marginal inhabitants: the alien, the immigrant, the rebel. Another family legend, worn with repetition: a journey o the new world fraught with turnings back, and multiple beginnings. Stein's paternal grandparents had arrived in America in 1841 from Germany; they belonged to what became known as the 'old immigration', from the countries of central and northern Europe. Her grandmother had led them there with a wagonload of their possessions. At one point on the journey to the ship bound for America she had looked back to find her husband had stopped in the road and turned homeward; she had to go back and urge him to continue trudging towards their family's glittering American future. Even with the self-conscious portentousness that accompanied so many similar journeys to the new world, Hannah and Michael Stein could never have known that their granddaughter would one day transform this story into her own historical beginning, a moment of epic struggle and conquest that became an American Genesis; that they would become symbolic progenitors of her vision of a new America – 'the old people in a new world, the new people made out of the old'.[11]

But in 1875, when that granddaughter was not yet a year old, her American family set sail back to the old world, back to the Europe of their fathers, and settled in Vienna, for the reason that Daniel Stein, that incontrovertible but easily distracted patriarch, for the time being had got it into his head that his children should be educated according to the best European methods.

In adult life Gertrude Stein would become a mesmerizing, magnetic speaker whose mellow Californian tones were remembered by many who met her, whose conversation was what created her fabulous reputation; her talk drew the crowds to her Saturday evening salons, when all the while her written work lay stacked unread in cupboards, and she was hard pressed to find anyone to publish it. Ebullient, garrulous from the start, the baby Gertrude first chattered in German. When she tried to speak English her bizarre sentences caused great hilarity among her family and she would become quite cross. These were only the first of many occasions on which her attempts at communicating her ideas would be misunderstood, and indeed laughed at.

Frequently in her autobiographies she made a point of emphasizing (strange and unnecessary though it might seem) that English was her mother tongue, as if to preempt detractors who thought that it was not. In *The Autobiography of Alice B. Toklas* she framed the same anxiety as a humorous anecdote: the one about the time she was paying for *Three Lives* to be published. An envoy, she claimed, came to see her from the publishers in New York; believing English must be her second language, they were concerned she had an insufficient grasp of its grammatical rules. When she answered the door the young man was embarrassed to find that she was American. Then, she explained, she had to persuade him to print the book the way she had written it, as she had done it that way on purpose. The story only really works with the knowledge that Stein by that time knew she could trust her readers to believe that *Three Lives* was a prescient masterpiece, of all her works the most widely trumpeted as a great and lasting accomplishment.

Back in 1878, when Gertrude was four years old, the family moved from Vienna to Paris for a year. She would later recall very little of this first visit to her adopted hometown. But when, during the First World War, the streets were empty of vehicles, there

Gertrude Stein, aged four.

seemed to be something in the atmosphere that she remembered: the smell of horse manure, she thought perhaps it was. She did not remember but loved to hear the story of a Parisian shopping spree; the five-year-old Gertrude returned triumphant to the USA decked out with a new sealskin coat, gloves and riding costume, and the proud owner of two talismanic objects that foretold her future scientific career: a microscope and a multi-part French history of zoology.

Her father having abandoned the particular educational theories that had taken them to Europe, the family's new home was in Oakland, California, a wealthy suburb of San Francisco. After a short stay in Baltimore, the trip to California became in her recollections an epic journey across the open country with vistas of 'Indians', a magical, perennially replenished hamper of food, and her sister's bright red ostrich plumed hat surreally blowing out of the window of the train into the desert. Her father was this type of man: he stopped the train to go and get it.[12]

Daniel Stein had not come to California as a prospector, as the generation before him had; he was already a self-made man, but he headed with his family out West as a pioneer of sorts. He invested in the San Francisco Stock Exchange and in street railroads, as well as property. Energetic, volatile, argumentative, a sympathizer with the northern cause during the Civil War, and an espouser of healthy outdoor living, he wanted his children to be 'individual and independent'.[13] But at the same time he placed restrictions on Gertrude's liberty which she resented. He was progressive, but a faddist, impatient, capricious and overbearing, particularly towards the meek and gentle Milly, his wife. To his children he could sometimes be frightening. 'Fathers are depressing', Gertrude succinctly, and repeatedly, noted.[14] His domineering attitude to her was a driving force in her desire to overcome heredity and find a different basis for the formation of character: 'living down the tempers we are born with'. Her idea of parenthood was, like many of her ideas of human relationships, rooted in antagonism. A scribbled note from 1903 which eventually became the epigraph of *The Making of Americans* emblazoned the late Victorian theme of intergenerational discord across her work:

> Once an angry young man dragged his father along the ground through his own orchard. 'Stop!' cried the groaning old man at last, 'Stop! I did not drag my father beyond this tree'.[15]

Cycles of aggression and repetition pervade her work. In *The Making of Americans* the relation between father and children involves 'mostly fighting'.[16] The father is angry, and psychologically violent. She refers to the children as 'big struggling children', with Darwinian significance, while the 'little gentle mother' is one of the casualties of evolution, who simply 'died away'.[17] In the novel Stein cast herself as Martha Hersland, the type of a vigorous, healthy American girl, perhaps in reaction to the memory of her mother's weakness and ailing health.

Oakland was the place of which Stein was to declare, when she returned in the 1930s: 'There is no there there.' But that was a comment on her own inability to recast herself as belonging in America, a sense of emptiness at the heart of her earliest experiences, an inability to reconcile herself with her own previous incarnation. Her San Francisco childhood was in fact a cultured one; here she first saw French painting, French plays. Roundly impressed by Millet's *Man with a Hoe*, she bought a reproduction, of which her brother Michael commented that it was 'a hell of a hoe'. To her it seemed the beginning of her aesthetic education, the first time she had noticed that art was a thing apart from reality, that it could be not just an emulation of real life but its own world.[18]

Gertrude, the baby of the family, was cosseted and petted. Michael, the eldest brother, was the family's rock; Gertrude treated her next two siblings with an attitude ranging from disinterest to disdain, and claimed that she never liked Bertha ('not a pleasant person'), while Simon was something of a simpleton.[19] Gertrude's ability to shrug off inconvenient family members when they failed to collude with her perception of her own genius would be echoed in later life in her abrupt terminations of many friendships. Gertrude and Leo, the two youngest, early developed a strong bond of affiliation, but Leo too would eventually fall by the wayside, and many luminaries would also feel her stony wrath; Virgil Thomson, the composer and friend with whom she collaborated on the opera *Four Saints in Three Acts*, once received out of the blue a card inscribed with the words: 'Miss Stein declines further acquaintance with Mr Thomson'.[20] Stein once asked the poet William Carlos Williams what he would do if he had as many unpublished works as she did. His reply was that as there were so many, he would probably select the best and throw the rest into the fire. 'The result of my remark was instantaneous. There was a shocked silence out of which I heard Miss Stein say, "No doubt. But then writing is not, of course, your métier."'[21] That was the precipitate end of another possible friendship. The shutting of her atelier door could be as abrupt as the opening of it could be magnanimous.

The young Stein was schooled in various ladylike accomplishments, but it was a wide open, Western, frontier world the family inhabited; she played the piano, but also knew how to use a gun. Both she and Leo were bookish and outdoorsy in equal measures. Books were at the centre of family life. Stein claimed that as a child she read Wordsworth, Scott, Bunyan, Shakespeare, 'congressional records encyclopedias etcetera' . . . everything she could get her hands on, indiscriminately: from Richardson's *Clarissa* to Carlyle's *Frederick the Great* and Lecky's *History of England*. When she was eight years old she decided to write a play, and got as far as an optimistic stage direction: 'the courtiers make witty remarks',[22] but was forced to abandon the endeavour after realizing she was unable to think of any witty remarks. (The telling of this story was both a pricking of her own pomposity and a subtle homage to her-self; 'witty remarks' had by then become her currency.) She and Leo, prudent collectors in the making, claimed that when they were in their early teens they bought books as security against the possibility of their family's drop in fortunes. Gertrude boasted that by the age of fifteen she was worried that the world was going to run out of good things for her to read. Gertrude and Leo also spent many long, happy days out trekking together in the rolling Californian hills. By the time they reached adolescence they were inseparable. 'We were born bohemians', wrote Gertrude only a few years later while at college, already staking out their mutual future.[23]

Stein always professed not to like highbrows and intellectuals. She celebrated ordinary people and aligned herself with the middle class. Belonging to the middle class, being normal, was a kind of lifelong disguise for someone as obviously eccentric and unusual as Stein; despite its implicit threat to her individuality, it was a label she could take refuge behind. She liked to make friends with any-one she came across, or perhaps it was that she liked to flaunt her friendships with mechanics, farmers and soldiers just as much as she name-dropped the aristocracy of the European avant garde. One rather smug, comic definition of democracy she later spun was that if you treat everyone equally anyone will do anything for you. Perhaps it was that Stein genuinely craved the freedom of classless-ness. Brought up by governesses and always waited on by maids and cooks, Stein set many of her stories among the servant popula-tion, in whose environment patterns of thought and speech seemed more open to experimentation. The debate surrounding the influence of immigrant servants who lived within the families of mainstream America, 'the servant girl question', was a heated one during Stein's girlhood. Many of her fictional servant girls are immigrants, or 'foreign', as she calls them. These foreign women's marginality seemed to imply to her a certain freedom from conven-tional lexical, and moral, codes of decorum.

From the start hers was a life of privilege, and in all her accounts of it she is careful to present herself as extraordinary, an incipient genius. As Martha Hersland, her alter-ego, grows older she is separated from the children around her by a kind of natural selection. Although her father has no regard for social distinctions based on wealth or class, her 'natural future' separates Martha from her poorer friends.

In *The Making of Americans* her description of her childhood home was a lyrical love poem, a bucolic paradise; it was also an image of wildness and entangled nature held within limits. Around the house was a hedge of roses – 'not wild, they had been planted'; there is an interest in breeding that links the exquisite roses with the rich people inside the fence.[24] The poor people pick the roses and the family set their dogs on them, but they return. This theft signifies a larger social tension; here is middle-class America assailed by the people on its margins. Artificial selection cannot entirely contain or suppress the growth in the garden; the roses continue to grow beyond the fence; the deviations and mutations, the pressing on boundaries are what constitute life itself. The traditional walled garden of the family is invaded by societal pressures.

The walled garden of Stein's childhood was, she always maintained, a happy place, and she would always stress the grand normality of her upbringing, but in 1885, aged ten, Gertrude began to realize that her mother's health was in decline; frail and gentle Milly had become an invalid. In 1888, when Milly finally succumbed to cancer, Gertrude was fourteen. In *The Making of Americans* Stein characterized her mother as a weak little thing, amenable but detached. Fifty years later in *Everybody's Autobiography* Gertrude's own willed detachment from the emotions of that period had gone so far that she was able to dismiss her mother's death, saying that the family 'all already had the habit of doing without her';[25] and in *The Making of Americans* she was able, chillingly, to claim that after her death the family 'soon forgot' her.[26]

In her work she would only ever allow herself to overcome that forgetting of being mothered in momentary glimpses, such as this scene of confusion from 'Possessive Case' (1915): 'I was trembling because my mother had never loved me and I circled about and I made a promise and I did lessen birds I showed the whole perturbation and believe me . . .';[27] such glimpses are torn apart and scattered and impossible to piece together.

When her mother died, Stein was going through what she called the 'agony' of adolescence; she later alluded to her fear of death, loneliness and a 'rather desperate inner life' at this time.[28] After Milly's death, in 1889 Daniel Stein became vice-president of a cable car line, the Omnibus Cable Company in San Francisco, and the business prospered. His sisters conspired to find him a new wife, but none of them were suitable. Did the family mourn her? Gertrude left no record of it, other than a lifelong hostility to what she saw as weak women.

The first story Stein ever wrote, as a sophomore at college, was called 'In the Red Deeps', evidently written at the time when she was 'still under the influence of George Eliot'.[29] (It was an influence, along with that of Henry James, under which she would labour, never achieving a successful voice until she completely broke free of her two literary heroes.) In her story, Stein offered a fairly frank description of her feelings of sexual frustration at this time. She describes lying in bed next to her sister, listening to her breathing, overwhelmed by urges about 'dreadful possibilities of dark deeds', with sadomasochistic hints, and a powerful 'fear of loss of self-control'.[30] Stein remembered this story as one of her few expressions of the torment of her adolescence. Her mother's death could not have come at a more crucial moment in her own development. But her response was to ignore or bury it. In her autobiographies she looked on the age of fourteen as a turning point, but was never explicit about why. She also implied that this was the time when she began to write, as a way of consoling herself for her 'disappointment and sorrow'.[31] What is striking is that there was disappointment before there was anything else. Her writing life was a way of trying to overcome a disappointment that had already engulfed her before she even began. Gertrude's relationship with Leo was, however, fortified by motherlessness. Leo was her only ally, their books her only source of external comfort. 'My mind from childhood was one which constantly fed on itself', she later wrote.[32] In 1890 she listlessly dropped out of the high school she had been attending for a year or so. Her formal education, at least until college, was patchy and subject to her father's whims.

The following year, Leo went to wake his father, and found him lying dead in bed, and as Gertrude matter-of-factly put it: 'Then our life without a father began, a very pleasant one.'[33] If her response to her mother's death had been muted and internalized, her response to her father's could hardly have been less sentimental. The abrupt end of childhood was a serendipitous way out of a life she had been longing to escape. On Daniel Stein's death each of the five children got $60,000 in property, stocks and cash. Thanks to big brother Michael's prowess at managing these investments and his franchise of the cable car company, Gertrude and the others would be financially independent for the rest of their lives, and none of them would ever have to work for a living: a situation that could indeed be described as 'pleasant'.

At seventeen, the orphaned Gertrude left California and moved to Baltimore, to live with her mother's family among 'a large number of those cheerful pleasant little people', her aunts and uncles, as she remembered them from the height of her 1930s grandeur and acclaim.[34] She later saw this as a humanizing experience. Meanwhile Leo had enrolled at Harvard, and it was not long before Gertrude joined him in Cambridge, Massachusetts, at first as a visitor. Then, a year later in 1893, she herself enrolled as a special student at Radcliffe, at that time known as the Harvard Annex, apparently by sending a single, persuasive letter in application to the Academic

Board, and despite her desultory formal education. Being without parents, and without a proper education to speak of, without a home, would be the starting point of her proud claims to being a self-made genius. This was where most of her recollections about being Gertrude Stein began.

Two

Stein was one of about 250 girls to enrol that year at Harvard's younger sister institution (founded in 1879). By the time she arrived, she was immediately able to identify an 'Annex Girl' type; these were some of the first of what would become known as New Women. To these proper, earnest Eastern ladies, in pursuit of high ideals, Gertrude was so Californian that she seemed almost a foreigner.[1]

Living in a boarding house and billing herself as a David Copperfield figure, the orphaned Stein was confronted with new standards of behaviour in this province of Eastern learning. The West had meant to her 'freedom, imagination and unconventionality'.[2] Here the New Women of the East saw her as rough, eccentric and uncivilized. They commented on her fatness, her uncouthness and her uninhibited sweating. She in turn found them repressed and emotionally dishonest. There was a muted undertone of anti-Semitism in the atmosphere of Harvard, and most of Stein's close friends were Jewish. Although in truth she learned to love Cambridge and became a popular student, her disdain for the American, 'Anglo-Saxon' college girl type – she saw them as a uniform, conformist type – would last her whole life. She immediately set about rising above them.

From the 1970s onwards a steady onslaught of feminist readings of Stein's work (involving a brand of post-war feminism entirely alien to Stein herself) ensured that her avant-gardism became overly connected with an explicitly feminist doctrine, without recourse to feminism's historical meanings for Stein. (Of course, her complete refutation of gender as an issue in her work has made it all the more enticing as a field of study.) At the end of the nineteenth century, feminism was far from homogeneous, and becoming ever less so, and Stein's involvement with the feminism of the turn of the century was engaged, but problematic to say the least.

Gertrude's daily 'themes' for her English composition class were the testing ground for her first attempts at fiction. William Vaughn Moody, the poet and dramatist, was her tutor for English 22; a previous graduate of the class was Frank Norris. In these, her first completed compositions, she gave vent to adolescent anxieties and frustrations in a conventional, naturalistic style. 'Books, books . . . Nothing given me but musty books', exclaims one autobiographical protagonist.[3] Another enjoys a secret moment of sensual pleasure as a strange man presses up against her in church. It's a muted scene of sexual rebellion, testing the constraints on feminine sexuality, of the kind that crops up in much New Woman fiction of the time.

Aside from offering insights into Stein's adolescent psychology, these early college pieces are not of much literary value, and are not particularly well written. She had a lackadaisical attitude to revisions, informing her tutor at the end of one piece that she would rather be at the opera. But they do express her doubts and dissatisfactions about the education system for women. In 'An Annex Girl' (12 December 1894), a brief, rather forlorn fragment, an Annex girl with an enormous head perched on a frail body collapses on top of a 'miserable little heap' of books. (In the light of Stein's subsequent career her tutor's comment in the margin seems prophetic: 'your vehemence runs away with your syntax.')[4] Taking a similar theme to somewhat more intemperate lengths, one of the most striking pieces is simply called 'Woman' (20 November 1894), in which the speaker offers an unfavourable definition of womankind: 'Never again will I (ever) try to reason with a woman', she

Stein, the medical student, late 1890s.

announces melodramatically. 'The eternal feminine is nice to be sure but it's painfully illogical.'[5]

Unreasonable, hysterical, repetitive, pigheaded, and above all illogical. When Stein wrote this she was twenty years old, studying at Radcliffe and living off family money after the death of both her parents. She had not yet read Otto Weininger's *Sex and Character*, which would further testify against this feminine illogicality by categorically equating it with immorality (and which would also rely on Nietzsche's idea of the 'eternal feminine'), but she had already decided that she did not want to be classed as a woman – just at the moment when technically she had become one. Her tutor's wry comment at the end of this piece – 'point of view nobly remote' – perhaps reveals an awareness of Stein's need to overcome her own illogical thinking. This was a time when she was struggling to make herself intelligible through the written word, in these daily 'themes'.[6] And this was the first appearance of what would become a persistent masculine authorial pose. By describing what a woman is, she automatically placed herself at a remove; in 1894 maturity, logical thinking, and the possibility of greatness meant masculinity for Stein. After this point she abandoned the creative writing course and her university career took a scientific turn; her scientific compositions would no longer require her to describe her own emotions, but would allow her free rein to dissect and evaluate the emotional lives of others.[7] It suited her to believe the scientific gaze was implicitly masculine, free of feminine emotion.

Here, then, was her first adoption of a male persona in her writing. In conversation and correspondence she became known as the 'father' figure in the little family of her circle of friends. Reconstructing those days, Stein would convert this masculine posturing into a typically eccentric, perversely cocky but revealing wisecrack about a friend who encouraged her to support women's suffrage, about which she was unenthusiastic: 'Not, as Gertrude Stein explained to Marion Walker, that she at all minds the cause of women or any other cause but it does not happen to be her business.'[8] Her reaction to the chauvinism she encountered in her university career and to the struggle to be considered in the same league as her male counterparts seems to have been to make a serendipitous leap of illogic, and place herself weirdly above the whole fray.

At Radcliffe Stein was known as an unconventional figure who sported a sailor's cap (the first of many items of debonair head-gear); spirited, confident, well liked, a keen talker, she became secretary of the philosophy debating club. Her teenage melancholy seemed to have been overcome; in its place was a warmth and a palpable enjoyment of life that drew people to her.

In 1895 Leo pulled out of Harvard Law School and went to New York, where he was drawn to a glamorous group of worldly-wise New Men, globetrotters, newspapermen, politicians and art collectors. He began his own travels; setting sail for Antwerp, his first European trip as an adult culminated in Paris, where he spent most of his time in the Louvre, honing himself as an art critic. On his return he was asked to play companion to the Steins' cousin Fred on a trip to Japan, where he became a connoisseur of Japanese art; and after that he started urging Gertrude to join him on his next jaunt, back to Europe.[9]

Gertrude, meanwhile, had plunged into the era of new sciences which branched out from evolution theory. Her major courses were in psychology, zoology and botany; among her tutors were William James, Josiah Royce, Hugo Münsterberg and George Santayana, all engaged in explaining the 'American mental quality',[10] as well as Charles B. Davenport, who was to become America's leading eugenicist. During this period Stein's lifelong interest in defining character solidified. That Stein trained as a psychologist and a zoologist in the laboratories at Harvard is of paramount importance to all her subsequent literary experiment.[11] Her scientific persona had a direct effect on her literary compositions. Mina Loy recognized this in her poetical tribute to Stein in 1924:

Curie
of the laboratory
of vocabulary
she crushed
the tonnage
of consciousness
congealed to phrases
to extract
a radium of the word[12]

In point of fact Stein was useless as a chemist. But her work in experimental psychology, neuropsychology and zoology, and then in the mapping of the brain that was going on at Johns Hopkins, gave her a unique relation, as a creative writer, to the science of her day.

When Stein first entered the Harvard Psychology Laboratory in 1893, the science itself was in its infancy. For the orphaned Stein, to whom so many doors were open, so many possibilities on the horizon, who saw herself springing into a new world in which the laws of the old were no longer necessarily applicable (she shared the common millenarian note of her era), psychology was a new science with which to classify that world, a system to grasp onto. And one of its fathers, that unconventional champion of liberated thinking, William James, was her teacher. His *Principles of Psychology*, one of the founding texts of the new science, had been published three years before Gertrude enrolled at Radcliffe. In her sophomore year Stein studied under James's protégé, Hugo Münsterberg, who wrote to her at the end of the year that she had been his 'ideal student'.[13] Münsterberg believed that every psychological occurrence had its basis in a physiological one. So satisfactory was Stein's first year's work of experimental psychology with him in the area of acoustics that she was invited the following year by James himself to take part in his seminars, and carry out experiments supervised by him in person.

Here is Stein's (perhaps apocryphal) note to Professor James at the top of an end of year exam paper, which she abandoned unwritten: 'Dear Professor James, . . . I am so sorry but really I do not feel a bit like an examination paper in philosophy to-day'; and his supposed riposte: 'Dear Miss Stein, I understand perfectly how you feel I often feel like that myself' – after which, she claimed, he gave her top marks, and she still got to go to the opera.[14] The anecdote distils a certain dilettantish attitude to her scientific career, but also a desire to present herself as a favourite of the great man. In her third year at Radcliffe, in 1896, under James's suggestion and guidance, Stein embarked on a series of experiments into automatism with her classmate Leon Solomons.

'Automatic writing' was at the time a favourite tool of mediums and spiritualists who claimed it provided a connection with the spirit world. William James himself was on famously equivocal and open terms with this spiritualist view of the mind's powers. But psychology officially considered automatic writing a door instead to the unconscious regions of human thought. Its use was particularly common in the treatment of hysteria, as hysterics were supposed to be more susceptible to allowing that buried 'second personality' to express itself.

Technically what Stein and Solomons produced was distracted writing.[15] They would read a novel and distractedly scribble sentences at the same time; or one of them would read a piece of writing while the other read something aloud to them, and they eventually achieved a state of mind that allowed them to carry out both acts simultaneously. The aim was to distinguish how the sort of ordinary, distracted acts that everyone performs every day, without paying attention to them, shaded into the so-called 'second consciousness' of the hysteric.[16] In other words, to show that what was attributed to that 'second personality' could be done by normal people in a distracted state, thereby disproving the theory of a second personality. By achieving a sort of dissociation from their own acts by distraction, Stein and Solomons summarized that hysteria was 'a *disease* of the *attention*'. This work was eventually published as 'Normal Motor Automatism'. In their joint publication Stein and Solomons write that they are 'both . . . perfectly normal – or perfectly ordinary';[17] by attributing normality to themselves they become assimilated within the objectivity, neutrality and universality claimed by contemporary science.[18] The question of what constitutes the 'normal' would be one which lingered in Stein's work ever after.

In 1934, when Stein's literary work had gained both popularity and notoriety, it was the subject of a critique by the psychologist B. F. Skinner, published prominently in *The Atlantic Monthly*, entitled 'Has Gertrude Stein a Secret?' Skinner claimed that, using the techniques of automatic writing, in *Tender Buttons* (published in 1914) Stein had invented a second personality for her narrator, one without a past or much intellect. Many readers followed Skinner into using automatic writing as an answer to the puzzle of Stein's more challenging techniques, her 'unintelligible' sentences. Couching their claims in fairly hostile if not outrightly misogynist language, critics not only claimed that Stein was a practitioner of automatic writing, but suggested that because Stein's poetry resembled its dissociated effects, it amounted to a proof of her own hysterical tendencies, her own 'degenerate' nature. It was a censorious view that linked the breaking of literary rules with moral laxity, a view of words themselves as morally diseased. It has been one of the most lingering myths surrounding Stein's work, though it has often been refuted.

Stein herself disputed the idea that any of her work was produced by automatic writing, and noted that she didn't even think what she and Solomons had produced in the laboratory could properly be classed as automatic writing – she didn't think it was possible under laboratory conditions. She said that 'writing for the normal person is too complicated an activity to be indulged in automatically.'[19] She did not believe, in fact, that unless one was hypnotized, it was possible to produce writing that did not in some way 'make sense'. How she described the result of the experiments was that 'A phrase would seem to get into the head and keep repeating itself at every opportunity . . . The stuff written was grammatical, and the words and phrases fitted together all right, but there was not much connected thought.'[20] Stein and Solomons had been looking for writing with nothing, no consciousness behind it – but there was, she later contended, no such thing. Speaking specifically about *Tender Buttons*, she told an interviewer: 'I made innumerable efforts to *make words write* without sense and found it impossible. Any human being putting down words had to make sense of them' (my emphasis).[21] That attempt at transference of agency to the words themselves, rather than the consciousness behind them, was an important admission. The removal of meaning from words had been part of the experiment of *Tender Buttons*; it just hadn't worked. She would continue to insist on exploring the freedom of words from meanings and antecedents: 'I like the feeling of words doing as they want to do and as they have to do', she later wrote.[22]

Stein and Solomons had, after all (with a certain amount of scientific naivety) used themselves as subjects. The lines that Stein produced in the experiment with Solomons showed, as they reported, 'a marked tendency to repetition' – later a characteristically 'Steinian' device – and some of them seem to sound pre-emptive echoes of her later style: 'When he could not be the longest and thus to be, and thus to be the strongest'.[23]

What Skinner disregarded in his attempt to discredit Stein's writing by noting the similarities of the finished product to automatic writing, and linking them to the outpourings of hysteria, was Stein's awareness of her own effects. She was bound to deny it, but there is little doubt that, although in later years she did not actively practice automatic writing, Stein was intrigued by the idea, and she was obsessed by the question of how writing is linked to consciousness.

Stein, with skull and microscope, late 1890s.

She became, with her background in psychology and neuropsychology, a powerful thinker and theorist on the relation of writing to the work of the brain, and her 'experimental' writing – perhaps the *most* experimental work produced by any writer of the twentieth century – depended on recognition of aspects of how writing works that are normally left implicit or unnoticed.[24] As Steven Meyer argues in his detailed study of the relation of Stein's scientific career to her creative writing, in doing so she not only absorbed scientific ideas into her writing, nor merely wrote in a spirit of scientific enquiry, nor simply used science as a metaphor, but made her creative writing itself into a kind of experimental science.[25] In science, the failure of one experiment could lead the practitioner on to further discoveries; so Stein included her failures in her work. In the midst of her most grammatically and verbally 'experimental' period, she wrote 'I see I have a trained eye I do microscopic work'.[26] Although she later tried to shake off the experimental model (in *Everybody's Autobiography*), this was partly to do with her reluctance to be called an 'experimental writer', a tag which seemed to suggest inferiority, a secondary status in the pantheon of literary greatness. She preferred to see herself as an inventor or, most of all, a genius.

Her experience of 'automatic writing' primarily instilled in her the new and radical perspective of seeing writing as an artefact, a product rather than a process, and gave her an idea of the words on the page as objects in themselves which need not necessarily be related to one another, a Saussurean realization of the randomness of the linguistic sign (although, of course, independently arrived at), a slippage of meaning in words as signifiers which could bring them into new relations with one another. Her attempts at removing meaning from words were both disconcerting and, eventually, liberating. In automatic writing, it was the physical process of the formation of words and word groupings by an independently moving pencil that supplied her with a new vision of the power of words as nothing more or less than words, writing as pure behaviour.[27] (One of Stein's hobbies was reading people's handwriting. In doing so, again, she was not looking at the meaning of the words on the page, but regarding them as objects which provided indirect clues to character.) It was also the first of her enquiries into 'How Writing is Written', which would become a pervasive theme of her own work. In the 1930s she would lecture on words and their relation to consciousness, the mind of words.

Later she would counsel a younger writer that: 'creation must take place between the pen and the paper', rather than in planned thought before composition.[28] (She had a lifelong disgust for typewriters.) She never denied the similarity in appearance between her work and so-called automatic writing; what she denied was the presence of the automatic element within herself.

In a theme written at the time of these experiments, Stein describes the physical experience of automatic writing as a form of torture: a girl is strapped into a sort of machine for writing,

> her finger imprisoned in a steel machine and her arm thrust immovably into a big glass tube . . . Strange fancies begin to crowd upon her, she feels that the silent pen is writing on and on forever. Her record is there she cannot escape it . . . her imprisoned misery.[29]

This is a striking extrapolation of the mechanical apparatus and processes of the laboratory into the psyche, via the action of writing. Writing itself becomes a source of distress. Just as the hydrocephalic, hysterical subject of her earlier theme 'An Annex Girl' had collapsed under the weight of books, here the girl is shut in the prison of her own hysterical composition. She was, in these themes, exploring not only 'The Value of College Education for Women' (the title of a speech she gave to a Baltimore Women's Group in 1898), but the value of contemporary scientific procedure: 'Before long this vehement individual is requested to make herself a perfect blank while someone practices on her as an automaton.' Stein was a 'vehement individual'; she did not easily succumb to the idea of herself as an 'automaton'. She would repudiate Skinner's claims four decades later for much the same reason.

The natural outcome for Stein of this adverse image of the hysterical woman writer was to abscond herself from the possibility of being included in it. As Stein put it in *The Autobiography*, she 'never had subconscious reactions'.[30] She made this doubly reassuring by couching it in a story about William James, in which she made her half-fictional James imply that whatever she did (however abnormal), it was normal: an all-satisfying, all-justifying claim. Paradoxically she wanted all her abnormalities to be wrapped up and cosseted in a vision of the normal that still allowed, indulged her individuality. Her interest in character was partly an egotistical urge to understand her own character, her own composition, at this time. 'I was tremendously occupied with finding out what was inside myself to make what I was.'[31] This included her relative masculinity or femininity. In her notebooks she described herself as a 'masculine type'.

The feminist debate of the period was tied in with the pseudoscientific definition of the very meaning of masculinity and femininity. Experimental psychology was the testing ground for Stein's ideas on this subject; later they would gain a shaky philosophical prop in Weininger's *Sex and Character*. Weininger's belief in women's particular susceptibility to hypnotism, and propensity to 'psychic automatism', an example of feminine lack of will, may have influenced Stein's claims that she was not a useful participant in automatic experiments (Weininger 'despised' the idea of a subconscious).[32]

Taking a much needed change of surroundings in the summer break after these experiments in 1896, Gertrude joined Leo in Antwerp; it was an archetypal literary-aesthetic tour for well-connected Americans in Europe. They toured Holland and Germany, Gertrude an eager apprentice to all her brother's theorizing about art, then fleetingly stopped in Paris, and then London for a month, which did not strike Gertrude favourably. When she returned to Radcliffe for her final year she would further develop her experiments in automatic writing, this time on her own, and this time she would combine them with her growing interest in character types.

Working this time without Solomons, the plan was to discover the susceptibility of various character types to automatic behaviour, not necessarily writing; to see how different types differed in their habits of attention. The subject's arm would be placed on a planchette hung from the ceiling; in their hand they held a pencil. Stein would talk or read to them, and when they seemed distracted by her words she would surreptitiously guide their hand, so that they would draw a shape on the paper. (The image of the student Stein manipulating her subjects' hands, while boldly attempting to peer into their minds, seems to foretell the mature Stein's domineering intellectual stance as the chronicler of writing's relation to consciousness.) She classified the results according to type. Most of the subjects were what she called the 'New England' type – which she classified as morbidly self-conscious. Type I were nervous, with strong powers of concentration. Type II were blonde, pale and emotional. They had poor powers of concentration, were suggestible, likely to produce automatic movement, and verging on the hysterical.[33] These ideas were published in the cutting edge journal *The Psychological Review* under the title 'Cultivated Motor Automatism': Stein's first printed work, since her earlier work with Solomons had been written up by him. Groping towards a scientific system for the basis of identity with a melange of ideas taken from morphology, physiognomy and typology, Stein described her work as a study of 'the nervous conditions of men and girls at college'.[34] She was already mapping out for herself a career as a doctor; she had a particular interest in nervous diseases in women (often related in the period's medical literature to sexual or reproductive disorders). Later her work would be cited in the hysteria section of Havelock Ellis's groundbreaking work of sexology, *Studies in the Psychology of Sex*.

Already this schematic arrangement of character traits suggests the system that would engulf Stein in her urge to catalogue every kind of person who ever could be living. Her scientist's eye was trained not to see an external governing force behind emotions and personality, but to see personality forged through habit and repetition. In *The Making of Americans* (written between 1903 and 1911), Stein offers a range of answers to the problem of what character is, or of what exactly it is constituted; the notion of 'kinds', then 'bottom nature', then 'being'; but its basis, even in her pursuit of a new literary language with which to cope with such ideas, is in experimental psychology, in finding physical phenomena to represent psychological ones, as Münsterberg had taught her.

> How quickly and how slowly, how completely, how gradually, how intermittently, how noisily, how silently, how happily, how drearily, how difficultly, how gaily, how complicatedly, how simply, how joyously, how boisterously, how despondingly, how fragmentarily, how delicately, how roughly, how excitedly, how energetically, how persistently, how repeatedly, how repeatingly, how drily, how startlingly, how funnily, how certainly, how hesitatingly, anything is coming out of that one, what is being in each one and how anything comes into that one and comes out of that one makes of each one one meaning something and feeling, telling, thinking, being certain and being living.[35]

Those persistent 'hows' both pose myriad questions and suggest that they have been or will be in some way answered. Stein poses as the scientific, egalitarian observer of character formation through habit, as if she has all the answers, but in fact she equivocates, or experiments, over and over again. Her adoption of an empirical, scientific viewpoint in the novel led her to devote several notebooks to laying out schemes and diagrams of types and their connections to one another. She scurrilously compiled judgemental sketches of the various types as visible among her friends.

While rejecting B. F. Skinner's analysis of her methods in relation to automatic writing, Stein did claim that the report 'Cultivated Motor Automatism' showed the first appearance of the style that she would develop in *Three Lives* and *The Making of Americans*. By this perhaps she meant the classification of types, the empirical method, the analytical approach, her view of character as a system of antagonisms (attacking and resisting, or various permutations of dependence and independence), and indeed the basis of these types in classifications ruled by sexuality. Sometimes in *The Making of Americans* she envisions character as a literal substance which moves and mutates:

> not . . . an earthy kind of substance but as a pulpy not dust not dirt but a more mixed up substance, it can be slimy, gelatinous, gluey, white opaquy kind of thing and it can be white and vibrant, and clear and heated.[36]

This is part of an ongoing sexual metaphor in the novel, an attempt to describe a polymorphous sexuality as the basis of character. Perhaps in response to her feelings about her own sexuality at this time, she was, like so many scientists, pseudo-scientists, and novelists of her era, querying to what extent such binary oppositions as male and female, masculine and feminine, are useful, or even possible.

Her taxonomic approach to character was also strengthened by her other major area of study at Radcliffe: zoology. At the end of her time at Radcliffe, Gertrude was preparing for admittance to Johns Hopkins Medical School, where she was to receive the physiological training to allow her to continue work in psychology. Before gaining admittance to Johns Hopkins, she was obliged to pass a Latin exam that was presenting her with interminable difficulties. Nevertheless in 1897, the summer before Johns Hopkins, she could not resist pressing ahead with an advanced course in embryology at the renowned Woods Hole Marine Biological Laboratory, collecting ctenophores and studying marine taxonomy. This was where her heart lay, in research, observation and classification. Her career seemed to have veered as far from literary creativity as could be possible; it would take a giant change of heart to effect the turnaround that took place – either that, or a giant redefinition of what she believed literature could be and do. It meant a deliberate turning away from 'sentimental' idioms, an absorption of the role of the scientist into that of the creative writer.

Anatomy, physiology, pathology and bacteriology, pharmacology and neurology: these were the new areas of study for Stein, the prospective doctor, when she entered Johns Hopkins Medical School in Baltimore, having finally nailed the Latin exam. She would remain there for more than four years, following up her time at the country's top psychology laboratory with a degree course at the country's top medical school. Gertrude (and Leo, who had come to live with her) moved into a house in Baltimore, where they were accompanied by another of those servants whose lives so fascinated her, a German housekeeper called Lena who indulged Gertrude's every whim, for which she would later be rewarded by being enshrined in two of Stein's stories: her name in 'The Gentle Lena' and her character in 'The Good Anna.'

At Johns Hopkins Stein specialized, as she described it, in 'the anatomy of the brain and the direction of brain tracts';[37] she was one of the first students of modern neurological technique. The idea of the synapse was introduced to the world during her first year at medical school.[38] Studying brain sections, slices from the brain of a baby aged a few weeks, her work was good enough to be published in Lewellys F. Barker's *The Nervous System and Its Constituent Neurones* (1899).

Here is part of her description, taken from that work, of the topography of the brain – a description of the nucleus of Darkschewitsch:

> The nucleus is more or less conical in shape . . . the commissura posterior cerebri . . . appears as a dorso-ventral bundle, solid in the middle, subdivided dorsally into an anterior (proximal) portion and a posterior (distal) portion, while ventrically it expands in the form of a hollow pyramid, which rests directly upon the nucleus.[39]

Compare this with the procedural attitude, the diagrammatic approach in her descriptions of character in *The Making of Americans*:

> A mass of being of the resisting substance very active at the surface and active inside toward the center only here and there . . . isolated spots in the central resisting mass . . . Of this last I am not yet absolutely certain.[40]

In later years Barker 'often wondered whether my attempts to teach her the intricacies of the medulla oblongata had anything to do with the strange literary forms with which she was later to perplex the world.'[41] The answer was that, of course, they did.

Stein's decision to study medicine was a bold one for the time, given that women doctors were very few, and this was a time of general debate over whether women were even fit to be doctors, which was also being played out in the work of the most prominent American novelists.[42] Stein had been discouraged from pursuing the profession by her own friends and family, who wanted her to settle down and start having babies instead. That was never on the cards.

Her first two years at Johns Hopkins were mainly occupied with laboratory research, in which she attained reasonably good marks.[43] But before the end of her third year her work began to slip. While in Baltimore, as part of her course in obstetrics, Stein was expected to fulfil a quota of attendance at births, and visited patients at home, for which she visited the city's poor quarters. These first glimpses of life among Baltimore's poor black inhabitants would surface in the emulation of black voices and experiences in the story 'Melanctha'.[44] But Stein did not take to the delivery wards; the realities of childbirth made her nervous. Her plan had been to specialize in nervous diseases in women while at Johns Hopkins, following on from her interest in hysteria at Radcliffe. But when she was given practical experience in a hospital for insane women, her reaction was, according to Alice Toklas, that she could not stand being around them.[45] Stein later claimed to have lost interest in the abnormal at medical school, saying she found normality far more interesting.[46] But she also wrote: 'I did not like anything abnormal or frightening.'[47] She had an aversion to being around disease that did not befit an apprentice doctor. She consequently seems to have developed mild hypochondria, and became so worried about her health – specifically, that there was something wrong with her blood – that she took the unusual step of hiring a welterweight to box with her. Sickening women in particular seemed to trouble her, most likely bringing to mind the unhappy days of her mother's illness. Her fantasies of normality, and her attraction to the bourgeois family of good breeding, held an unspoken horror of a link between maternity or reproduction and illness, particularly nervous illness, which with a twisted logic provided further proof to her of femininity as a stumbling block to creativity. She claimed, when she said that remembering oneself as a child ruptured the world, that one way to regain that feeling of 'the everlasting', of the permanence of one's identity, was to make babies, to procreate.[48] The other way of course, if that option was not open to her, was to write, to create. To be a genius. In *Lectures in America* she spoke about the 'everlasting feeling' that composing sentences gave her. It was her hold on the world, and on herself.

In 1900 Gertrude and Leo sailed again to Europe, this time taking in Italy and Paris, where they attended the Grand Exposition. This was the very time and place at which Henry Adams's mind was famously boggled by new technologies, leading him to define the spirit of the modern, mechanistic age in 'The Dynamo and the Virgin'. The young Stein left no such prescient record of her visit, and it would be another few years before she had her own Parisian epiphany.

In Stein's final year at Johns Hopkins, she failed her course in obstetrics. It was to prove the stumbling block that meant she was never awarded her medical degree. On her return from the European trip, all Stein's experience in obstetrics and with nervous and reproductive diseases, as well as her peculiar animus against the American college woman, came together in a remarkable and perplexing essay she wrote on 'Degeneration in American Women'.[49] Here Stein addressed the problem of the declining birth rate in America with nationalistic zeal, as if the progress of America were literally a race against the old world. She placed the onus of responsibility with women, particularly educated women, who, she suggested, were neglecting their womanly duties and unpatriotically contributing to the downfall of American civilization by pursuing education instead of following their duty to reproduce.[50] In a remarkably reactionary declamation for someone in her position, it was as if she felt women's education were somehow a decadent pursuit. She employed threatening language about the weakness and degeneration of the individual bodies of such educated women, threatening in turn the constitution of America, as she saw it. Her argument was that women should stop attending to their own education and attend to the future of America. Anything else was 'degenerate'.

It can't have been straightforward for Stein to make these claims, given the struggles she herself had faced to reach the stage she was now at. Classes at the medical school were mixed, though the majority of students were male. The recollections of her male classmates tend towards unflattering accounts of her physical appearance. Stein, they also remembered with some disbelief, stood up to one of her professors, who enjoyed telling lewd stories and upsetting the female students. She also insisted that if she was being considered on an equal footing with her male colleagues, she had the right to examine men with venereal disease, something usually denied the female students.[51] She always enjoyed a fight.

She was in a position of conflict. Stein wanted to be a genius. She seemed to think that she could become one by an act of will.

But all the evidence around her convinced her that genius was the province of maleness. Rather than pressing on with female solidarity, she found a convoluted and idiosyncratic way of solving the problem for herself, by setting herself apart, and at the same time justifying her own lack of a maternal instinct. Femininity, she baldly stated, was to concern itself with increasing the birthrate. (She made a point of noting that there would, of course, be a handful of women in each generation who proved the exception to the rule.[52]) Other college women, those whose 'natural' destiny was to reproduce, were by definition not capable of genius. But Gertrude already knew that she was not destined to be a mother. She had begun mixing with sophisticated women from Bryn Mawr College, women who could show her aspects of her own personality, and sexuality, that she had not confronted before. This seems to be the time when Stein first became sexually active in her affairs with other women, though there is no record of individual early dalliances.[53] As a lesbian, she was implicitly raising her own status, making way for her own exceptionality. Just as she saw herself as both bourgeois and outré, normal and unique, she was the exception that proved the rule: a woman and a genius. A woman, as she characterized herself, with the attributes of maleness. Among these strained contortions of logic, this was hardly a very assertive attitude to her own lesbian identity, but it is the one that suited her for the time being. This was a time when the woman suffrage debate was at its most heated, and Stein was, essentially, expressing a wish to be like a man,[54] rebuilding herself in a more ideal version as she would throughout her life.

But she was scared of her own morbidity and the hysterical sort of distractedness that had infused the autobiographical characters in her college themes. She had also had a glimpse of the world of art that was luring her towards another future. Leo, the family's artist manqué, was by this time planning on settling in Europe. Gertrude's work began to suffer. For whatever reason, Stein did not complete her medical degree. Her planned internship at the Massachusetts State Hospital for the Insane was not to be. Apparently she told friends at the time she didn't care about the degree, but these other women students felt badly for her and for feminism.[55] Nearly forty years after the event, in *The Autobiography* she tells the story of quitting medical school. When the more progressive of her friends upbraid her in the name of 'the cause of women', she languidly retorts: 'you don't know what it is to be bored'.[56] Here Stein painted herself once again as above her peers, the egregious, somewhat supercilious possessor of a manifest destiny. In reality she was far less certain that such a destiny awaited her. She had, purely and simply, failed to get her medical degree; eight years of training at Radcliffe and Johns Hopkins had been for nothing. Her fear of future failure was understandably vivid and intense.

In July 1901 Gertrude was again in Europe. Joyfully reunited with Leo, she travelled with him to Spain and North Africa, and then again to Paris in August. By autumn she was back in Baltimore. Leo stayed on in Florence, where he planned to live. Gertrude, his little sister, had been his avid companion through childhood, adolescence and adulthood. He had once led Gertrude to Harvard; he would now lead her, through various stops and starts before a permanent rooting took place, to Europe and to their mutual discovery of modern art.

When one of her professors offered her the chance of a retake, this is how she claimed to have snubbed it:

> You have no idea how grateful I am to you. I have so much inertia and so little initiative that very possibly if you had not kept me from taking my degree I would have, well, not taken to the practice of medicine, but at any rate to pathological psychology, and you don't know how little I like pathological psychology, and how all medicine bores me.[57]

But this was another retrospective fantasy; in reality she did want her degree enough to return to Johns Hopkins and attempt to complete some extra research so that it could be awarded. But feeling the pull of other influences, eventually she presented a model of a brain that was so intricate and bizarre in its wrongness that it seemed a deliberate, final throwing over of her medical career. On seeing it, the world's greatest anatomist of the time, Dr Franklin Mall, remarked: 'Either I am crazy or Miss Stein is.'[58]

As this was also the time when Stein was experiencing her first sexual relationships with other women, and developing confidence in her own sexuality, this multitude of new excitements and anxieties found a way into her fiction. For this was also the period when she began to write in earnest. She dashed off a final article on the brain stem which was sent to the *American Journal of Anatomy*, and then abandoned her scientific career forever, in the same fell swoop that she abandoned America itself. The crossover with her literary career would be evident in the analytical title of her first sustained piece of fiction, *Quod Erat Demonstrandum* (*QED*).

Because for now, Gertrude had a more pressing concern. What she was discovering among these transatlantic sojourns was first love. Unwittingly she had become involved in a love triangle when she fell for May Bookstaver, a feminist and a femme fatale of Bryn Mawr. May was already entangled in an unspecific way with another young woman of Stein's acquaintance, Mabel Haynes. Gertrude was infatuated with May and suspicious of Mabel. Mabel was wary of Gertrude, and knew something was going on with May. May seemed to want to have her cake and eat it too. It was hopeless and passionate, and fraught with regret almost from the start. In *QED*, the *roman-à-clef* Stein wrote about the affair, there is a rapturous record of a kiss that 'seemed to scale the very walls of chastity'.[59] Stein was due to be disappointed in May's unwillingness to show her the same devotion.

Safe to say Stein's infatuation caused a rift with another friend, Emma Lootz, who heartily disapproved of the relationship and chastised Gertrude for it, though whether on grounds of its lesbian nature or on the grounds of a personal dislike of May is unclear. In Lootz's mind, as in the minds of many at the time, there was a confusion between the terms of a passionate friendship or unconsummated crush, and recognition of love between women as a serious thing deserving of respect. It was a confusion that was widespread, and such confusion partly allowed lesbian relationships to go unremarked upon, taken, at least on the surface, by the world at large as close friendships, if perhaps tacitly acknowledged as sexual relationships. But such confusion also makes Stein's attempt to describe it more complex and tortuous.

By this time Stein had apparently already had romantic relations with other women, and there was a relative openness about homosexuality within her circle. But the enforced secrecy (because of Mabel, the third member of the triangle, as well as May's parents) and the fervour of Gertrude's attachment to May, despite the cruelties that the latter seemed able to inflict, found its way into furious love letters, fragments of which survive in the original, and some of which were transcribed directly into *QED*. The plot of *QED* is melodramatic, and its style discursive, faux-Jamesian; much of it consists of painful, convoluted, self-justifying conversations between Adele (Gertrude) and Helen (May). Stein/Adele operates under a rather melancholy lesbian persona, aware of the hopelessness of the situation but unable to stop herself from feeling the way she does.

Loving May had driven her to despair, and plunged her back into the depression she had seemed to have overcome. Writing it was a catharsis. Shortly after she completed the novella, both May and Mabel married themselves into conventional respectability. The manuscript then sat in Stein's cupboard for nearly 30 years. Just as a work like Hilda Doolittle's *HERmione* could not be published during her lifetime, and other lesbian coming of age stories also failed to see the light of day at the time of their composition,

QED is a record of lesbian love at a time when such records, and such feelings, could not be made public. Even when, in 1930 or 1931, Stein 'found' it (claiming she had completely forgotten ever having written it), she shyly presented it to a friend to be read, and shyly asked if it might be publishable. *QED* looks tame now, but the answer was probably not – because of its subject matter, a lesbian romance – and in fact the book was not published until another twenty years had passed, in 1950, four years after Stein's death.

QED also offers evidence of Stein's self-perception as a young adult. 'I always did thank God I wasn't born a woman'; this is more masculine posturing, although also a reference to Jewish prayer.[60] The adversarial nature of the triangular relationship in *QED* would be repeated over and over again in Stein's early fiction. But never again would she write in such a straightforward, open and representational way about her own lesbian experiences. Later, perhaps with a savvier eye to publication, a more worldly-wise understanding of how the public viewed female homosexuality, and a happier sex life, she would make her lesbian content far more oblique, and express distaste for any writing that was overtly sexual. She had, however, established a pattern of discerning personality based on the way that people reacted with one another, and specifically based on sexual relationships.

In 1902, at the tail end of Gertrude's ill-fated romance, the Steins were once more in Europe, moving from Italy to England, and getting further depressed by the weather and the 'drunken women and children' in London. A highlight of their six-month stay in Bloomsbury was a meeting with Israel Zangwill. Stein's main impression of London was a nightmarish vision of gloomy streets and pimply-faced women, all in all an 'ugly surface'.[61] She spent most of her time at the library of the British Museum, reading copiously. It was at this time that she embarked on her ambitious project of reading her way 'through English narrative writing from the sixteenth century to the present'.[62] As she did so she copied down the names of these books, and her favourite passages, into notebooks kept over the next few years; hundreds of titles appear in them, including diaries, biographies and autobiographies. Indeed, although she stripped her experimental work of referentiality and context, and although she sometimes liked to claim that her genius was *sui generis*, it is worth remembering that she did herself a kind of disservice in making that claim; she was, in fact, extremely well read. After Gertrude took a trip back to New York, in June 1903 she was back in Paris, and it seemed like a breath of fresh aesthetic air. It was in Paris, at 27 rue de Fleurus in October 1903, that Gertrude finished *QED*, and put a definitive ending to her love affair, even if the book itself ended on an equivocal and mournful note. She made another brief visit back to the USA in Spring 1904, and then Gertrude joined Leo in Paris. She protested that she would be going back to America every year. But in fact she was in Paris for good. It would be 30 years before she made it back to America.

When she put aside *QED*, Stein was already at work on another composition; beginning to take form was a story about American character, 'The Making of Americans', which would after years of work become the novel of the same name. Early notes for the book, jotted down in 1903, deal with Stein's conflict between her attachment to America and the appeal of the old world. In the end she would conclude that 'Your parents' home is never a place to work.'[63] In this early version of her epic modernist saga, Stein wrote: 'we fly to the kindly comfort of an older world accustomed to take all manner of strange forms into its bosom'.[64] Paris would become just that comforting alma mater for a heartbroken eccentric on the cusp of thirty who had, as yet, failed to come up with any proof of her genius.

Three

Loosening her stays in the most literal as well as metaphorical of ways, de-corseting herself long before it was the fashion, soon after she arrived in Paris Stein slung out the tightly buttoned dresses she had compressed herself into at Radcliffe, and adopted another 'costume', as she called it. The originality of her dress – her loose-fitting, brown corduroy robes and voluminous kaftans; a lapis lazuli pendant round her neck and sandals on her feet – contained a large element of performance. On the streets of Montparnasse she became a recognizable eccentric; the Stein persona was being born. She began marketing herself even before she had written any writing to market. Over the years she would veer between dressing like a monk and dressing like a Roman emperor, both of which were images she actively cultivated. In 1928 when she made a triumphal entrance at the party held by Eugene and Maria Jolas for the contributors to *Transition*, she managed to combine both pomp and asceticism. She appeared, as Kay Boyle described her in *Being Geniuses Together*, 'in a severe and nunlike dress of purple silk',[1] while the throng cleared a passage for her procession to an awaiting chair, around which kneeled a half-circle of her acolytes. James and Nora Joyce were apparently the only people in the room oblivious to her splendid presence, and they made a great point of showing it.

When she first arrived in Paris, this icon of the Left Bank wasn't even sure about whether to stay. Her first love was gone by; in her

Outside 27 rue de Fleurus, *c.* 1907.

compositions she still laboured under a very conventional style, and she was dogged by depression and indecision.[2] *QED*, as much as it had helped her clarify her own sensual desires, had also been a laying out of all her vacillations and weaknesses of character. She had confronted her own sexual cowardice while admitting 'a passionate desire for worldly experience'.[3] In the previous three years she had made the long journey between the USA and Europe four times, and in the struggle over whether to stay or go, Paris finally won by default: it took her far enough away from the scene of her lost love. Her love for Paris, though not immediate, was deep and lasting.

Hers was a self-imposed exile that led to an intellectual rebirth. In Paris Stein was free to make herself anew as a worldly individual, and her decision to throw off the traditional cultural garb of femininity coincided with her decision to innovate in her writing:[4] the persona and the writing seem inextricably linked. All the same, it was not an immediate transformation. As Adele, her protagonist in *QED*, says: 'All I want to do is to meditate endlessly and think and talk',[5] a prophetic vision of Stein's role in the 'Paris experiment'.[6]

The place Leo had found at 27 rue de Fleurus was a four-room, two-storey apartment with an atelier attached, in a neighbourhood near the Luxembourg Gardens that was then not very fashionable, but popular with artists because the rent was cheap. The square drawing room with its high ceilings and whitewashed walls was filled with dark oak Renaissance furniture that Leo had picked up for a song in Italy, and at first with Leo's Japanese prints. In a matter of months these gave way to the most illustrious collection of modern art then in existence. In 1904 the Steins saw their first Cézannes, and started buying. Soon their walls would also be graced by Toulouse-Lautrec, Gauguin, Manet and Renoir, as well as Vallotton and Bonnard, all unframed and jostling for position in a place that was never meant as a gallery but had become, by dint of Leo's perspicacity, the world's first museum of modern art.[7] (When Leo moved out, Gertrude Stein and Alice Toklas would irreverently fill the place with kitsch knick-knacks, 'polychrome saints' and alabaster doves.[8])

Lonely, embittered and dependent in those early Paris years, Stein was recalled by early visitors to the rue de Fleurus as an imposing but quiet figure, taking everything in, but not advancing her own ideas, content to let Leo rule the roost. Stein's directness, her daunt, was already there – her petulance, her formidable conversation and her imperious self-confidence were things of the future.

Setting up home again with Leo was partly a necessity, and may have seemed the only viable financial option. Despite their later reputation as wealthy American collectors, neither of them was hugely well off; they merely bought judiciously. In that she remained dependent on her family's stipend, Stein was not really a woman of independent means. That she was not making her own way in life meant perhaps that her adult responsibilities were postponed. But as a result of this expedient co-habitation with her brother, what she found in Paris, almost by chance, was freedom from the anxiety of influence that might have stifled her at home.[9] Away from America, there was also nobody to expect her to get married and have children, the fate that had befallen May Bookstaver and Mabel Haynes and other women like them. Paris was already known by reputation as the international capital of lesbian love.[10] The city that had drawn Leo, and that Gertrude found when she joined him, was still draped, at least in the imagination of those who went there, in the vestiges of fin-de-siècle decadence, while parts of it were very slowly being colonized by monied bourgeois Americans. The artistic and social elitism of the old salons of the Faubourg St-Germain was being challenged by a new generation of creative minds. Belle Epoque Paris represented, and truly offered, freedoms – sexual, social, artistic – that were still hard-won back home in America. That was at the root of Stein's conviction, after thirty years of living there, that 'America is my country, but Paris is my hometown.' It was a new kind of home.

Later she would use the city itself as a part of her public image, when going to Paris – for a certain breed of young American – would mean a trip to visit Gertrude Stein. Many of the most memorable images of Stein show her on the streets of Paris. She seems to have been on the lookout for networking opportunities as soon as she arrived. She was drawn to those who could enliven her drawing room, and in this respect was a natural salonière. She wanted at first to listen to them talk. Afterwards she would write it all down. Her work is full of conversation, not just the tittle-tattle of memoir, but as the basis of her style: in 'Melanctha''s speech rhythms, in the snippets of conversation that flood through the portraits, right up until the dialogic structure of her last book, *Brewsie and Willie*. Everybody was a subject. As Paul Bowles commented some 30 years later on being taken under her broad wing: 'It did not take me long to realise that while I undoubtedly had her personal sympathy, I existed primarily for Gertrude Stein as a sociological exhibit.'[11] Since the days with her Baltimore aunts, she was capable of strenuous sociability, and found solitude almost unbearable. A living arrangement that allowed continual flow of guests, where her home became a social space, meant Stein had found her ideal environment, and made Paris her perfect backdrop.

Living with Leo was a domestic arrangement that diverted questions about her sexuality, and allowed her to do as she pleased behind a thin veil of conventionality. They were known, cattily, as 'the happiest couple on the Left Bank', and some visitors actually left with the impression that Gertrude was Leo's wife. It was a half-way house; a blueprint of an alternative lifestyle, the 'bohemian' lifestyle she would come to symbolize. Her mutually dependent relationship with him was a step towards the unconventional home life she would continue with Alice Toklas. At the rue de Fleurus Stein converted her anxiety about her own strangeness into a realignment of her own 'respectability'. It wasn't only an outward transformation: she ditched her past enthusiasms, and latched onto Leo's new ones, filtering everything to see how it might have a bearing on her new chosen path to greatness, as a writer.

Like his father, Leo was a talker and an espouser of theories – his nervous character, erratic enthusiasms and pedagogical leanings often made him difficult company. He offended dinner guests by belittling their opinions. He riled Matisse by trying to teach him about art. He was obsessed with his own nervous disorders and dysfunctional digestive system. He fancied himself as a great painter, which he was not, so he turned to art criticism, at which he excelled. Before Gertrude Stein found her voice, it was his talk that drew visitors to the rue de Fleurus; Leo's artistic perception was profound and influential. It is a reminder of the importance of oral culture and social interaction in the period that although his only two books of art appreciation were not published until 1927 and then 1947 (just before he died), his practically unrivalled insight made him one of modern art's most important early patrons and impresarios. He was also for 35 years Gertrude Stein's greatest companion, and the person to whom she still looked for guidance in everything.

As compulsively and impertinently as Leo talked, Gertrude wrote. As she settled into her new life Stein diverted herself by categorizing her friends, old and new, in terms of their romantic leanings. The first piece of writing she turned to after *QED* was another mannered novella, this time distilling her ideas about the American college woman, and recounting the complicated love life of her glamorous New York acquaintance Alfred Hodder, 'the Byron of Bryn Mawr'.[12] Hodder, who also visited the Steins in Paris, was involved in a scandal over an extramarital affair with Mamie Gwinn, an ethereal English lecturer. Unfortunately Gwinn was already involved with Martha Carey Thomas, the first Dean of Bryn Mawr. This story fascinated Stein, partly because of its echoes of the love triangle she had found herself stuck in. She turned it into *Fernhurst*, a story about a man on the brink of thirty who was already a failure. It was a story, Stein wrote (with very modern frankness), about 'the deepening knowledge of life and love and sex'.[13] Stein was fascinated by Hodder and his sexual ethics, doomed as he was, in her opinion, by an uneasy coupling of the chivalry of the old world and the liberties of the new. Hoping to avoid the weaknesses of character with which Hodder had scuppered himself, in her twenty-ninth year, she defined the aging process as the exchange of 'a great dim possibility for a small hard reality'.[14] It was a combination of pessimism and stoicism that would characterize the work of her belated maturity, but it seems ironic now that on the verge of her own 'golden age' she should have felt so forlorn. She could not have foreseen the embarrassment of intellectual riches that was about to come her way.

If any one event in Stein's new Parisian life represents a genuine turning point, it must be the 1905 vernissage of the autumn salon, at which she first saw the group of painters who would become known as 'les Fauves' (the wild beasts), in a term coined after this show. In her own story of her life she heralded this as her Henry Adams moment. Matisse's *Femme au Chapeau* was on exhibit at the autumn salon. It now seems an unlikely cause for scandal – a portrait of a woman wearing an enormous hat – but this great sprawl of green, red and violet paint was so radical, so shocking, and to some so ridiculous, that the *Woman with the Hat* was to become a potent symbol of the modern movement. In her account Stein writes that people were so offended by it that they tried to scrape the paint off with their fingernails, while she stood calmly by; the only thing that troubled her was that she was unable to see why other people were so angered by this painting, as to her it seemed so natural. By 1932, when she was recounting the event for mass consumption as part of the curious myth of her own rise to glory, Matisse was acknowledged as a modern master. She assumed a connection between the unintelligent, barbarian clawing at his painting and people's uncomprehending reaction to her own writing, thus firming up her allegiances with the great, and most importantly with the egregiously modern. Throughout her life Stein would dwell upon the destructive energy of the twentieth century, its need to 'kill' the nineteenth century; it was her calmly patricidal refrain.

The violence of the public reaction to *Woman with the Hat* was a shock for the penniless Matisse family; when the Steins made their momentous purchase of the painting it was nothing short of a lifeline. From then on the Steins made rapid acquisitions and the works amassed prodigiously. Simultaneous with their purchase of their first Matisse was their first Picasso, *Jeune Fille aux Fleurs*; they bought several more Matisses including his *Blue Nude*, and a flush of paintings from Picasso's Blue and Rose periods, the latter including *Young Acrobat on a Ball* and *Boy Leading a Horse*, which took pride of place in the atelier, along with Cézanne watercolours and several modern nudes including those by Renoir, Bonnard and Manguin, and pictures by Gauguin, Degas, Delacroix and Toulouse-Lautrec. The quantity of flesh on display did as much to create the outrageous reputation the Stein collection was gaining as did the way in which it was painted. By 1906 anyone who wanted to see the best and most sensational in modern art was obliged to visit the rue de Fleurus. Paintings were lit by gaslight and so squashed onto every available inch of the walls that those high up could hardly be seen, and sometimes those beneath had to be scrutinized with the aid of a lighted match held up to the canvas. As quickly as the paintings amassed, so did the people. At first those who came were a small coterie – the Matisses and a few other artist and writer friends. Later they had to move the collection into the pavilion next door; although the atelier was fairly large it was not designed to be a meeting place for all of avant-garde Paris. Gertrude Stein wrote nonchalantly about how the Steins' 'Saturday evenings' began. Bothered by the constant interruption of people clamouring at their door to be shocked by the new, or to be part of it, Gertrude and Leo decided it would be a good idea to invite visitors to attend at a set time. This would become the most famous artistic salon in Paris.

Much has been written about the relation of Stein's writing to modern art, not least by Stein herself. Perhaps the most significant creative relationship of her life was that with Picasso, whom she characterized with typical, teasing, affectionately snobby humour as a 'good-looking bootblack'.[15] The collision of this Californian malcontent and the aspiring Spanish genius happened in 1905, when Picasso was 24 and Stein was 31. He had emerged from his Blue period into his Rose period, full of harlequins and figures from the Cirque Medrano, where Picasso, according to Stein, went once a week, and where Stein herself was sometimes to be seen. By the winter of 1905–6 Stein was sitting for Picasso's portrait of her, writing the stories that would become *Three Lives*, and continuing with her long novel *The Making of Americans*. Later, keen to advertise her relationship with Picasso, in *The Autobiography of Alice B. Toklas* she blithely put words in his mouth, words which tried to exert a monopolizing hold on the genius of modern painting, at a time when their friendship was on the wane. She has him refer to her as his 'only friend',[16] and in the space of one sentence claims that Picasso's portrait of her is the origin of Cubism, and her own short story 'Melanctha' is the first modern short story.[17]

Overbearing self-aggrandizement (partly a rhetorical device) was something Stein became famous for, but how else should she respond to the fact that when she arrived in Paris there was an artistic revolution in process, and she was at its very centre? There was no permanent gallery where people could see Matisse and Picasso at this time, other than the Steins' living room; her brother, Leo was 'the leading patron of the most radical regeneration in painting since the Renaissance'.[18] Gertrude and Leo Stein were, at a critical time, Picasso's main patrons; as his first collectors, they subsidized his work by paying him a regular stipend. Gertrude in particular was his unflagging promoter; she advanced his cause among wealthy friends and acquaintances – anyone who would listen – and moreover persuaded them to buy his work. Meanwhile Stein's other brother Michael and his wife were responsible for the first works of Matisse and Picasso crossing the Atlantic; they brought modern art to America, and in 1906 it was the Steins who first introduced Matisse and Picasso to one another. Gertrude Stein was present at most of Leo's major purchases and continued buying without Leo when, with the advent of Cubism, Leo dismissed Picasso, calling both his work and Gertrude's an 'abomination'. At one time or another she sponsored Picasso, Matisse, Juan Gris (her second-best friend, according to the autobiography), Georges Braque and Francis Picabia. The prolific rival collector, the Russian millionaire Sergei Shchukin, whose formidable private collection in Moscow would later be confiscated and taken to the Hermitage, would come and discuss purchases with Gertrude Stein.

(When he saw Picasso's epochal *Les Demoiselles d'Avignon* at the rue de Fleurus, as Gertrude gleefully reported it: 'he said almost in tears, what a loss for French art.'[19] In contrast to Leo, who fell into fits of mocking laughter in front of it.)

The Steins' Saturday nights were indispensable for Picasso. He was depending on Leo and Gertrude's money – to live, and to rent a second studio in which to work – but the cachet of appearing on their walls alongside Matisse, Gauguin, Cézanne, Renoir and Manet was invaluable. It was undoubtedly a self-serving relationship for each; Picasso attracted people to Stein, but Stein helped make Picasso famous. In reality the point of intersection for Stein and Picasso came when they were young, and as they got older they grew apart (though they remained friends until her death). However, their shared youth was an extraordinary time, and theirs was an extraordinarily deep friendship which grew from an immediate recognition of affinity. The artistic alliance that Stein keenly played up was no piece of fakery.

Quite apart from finding in her his protectress, there is no doubt that the portrait Picasso painted of Stein was remarkably important to his development. Far from over-egging this in the autobiography, Gertrude Stein tells the story of Picasso's *Portrait of Gertrude Stein* with languid wit, and a Twainian, deliberately simple-sounding: 'they do not either of them know how it came about. Anyway it did.'[20]

By the time she wrote *The Autobiography* (1932) Stein was very good at creating an image of her own cultural significance by stressing her importance to male artists and writers. It became a pattern in her career, and it worked; it is now a commonplace to link Stein's writing with Picasso's painting, though his work is less immediately associated with hers: with the woman, yes – with the writer, hardly at all. Picasso confessed that he never understood Stein's work. Their mutual influence was at the level of personal rapport and exchange of ideas. There is a question about how detailed their aesthetic dialogues can have been, considering that when they met their only common language was a limited French in which neither of them were yet great or even adept conversationalists. But over 80 or 90 sittings, after three months of staring at each other, a mutual fascination and allegiance grew. In Picasso Stein had met a friend with whom she could trade analogies to her craft.[21] Picasso, she felt, was an equal, and importantly for her he was a male one. And Stein was making her own portrait while Picasso was painting his. As she later wrote: 'She had come to like posing, the long still hours followed by a long dark walk intensified the concentration with which she was creating her sentences.'[22] During the sittings, Stein was composing 'Melanctha', and Fernande Olivier, Picasso's lover, as Gertrude became her confidante, gave more than a little of herself, her languid sensuality and proud demeanour, to that character.

Every afternoon Stein made her way up to Picasso's studio in the Bateau-Lavoir, and on Saturdays he and Fernande might accompany her back to the rue de Fleurus for dinner and conversation, and so the Stein salons prospered; when Picasso entered the Steins' circle he brought his friends, and so enlarged and changed it. Those he brought along included the crowd of writers and artists who already got together at the Closerie des Lilas in Montparnasse, including the poets Max Jacob and Guillaume Apollinaire. More and more visitors began to come, to see the people as well as the paintings. The Saturday evening meetings would start at 9 o'clock and go on until the early hours.

The self-confidence, the impudence of the American siblings in setting themselves up as the authority on the new art movement in Paris can hardly be overstated. Their cosmopolitanism and a certain outcast status worked in their favour – the pair were disdained by genteel acquaintances, and banned from the Café Royal[23] for not wearing proper shoes (even though their sandals were made by Isadora Duncan's brother). Their salon became a meeting place for artists and writers of different nationalities and backgrounds, where niceness and propriety could be left at the door; this was no snobby institution. For one thing, although they were seen as 'the Stein corporation' for their mercantile prowess, the Steins could not afford to be snobby. And as Gertrude wryly put it in later years: 'I don't mind meeting anyone once.'

In the early years, Blaise Cendrars, Robert Delaunay, Matisse's friend André Derain, Georges Braque, Juan Gris and Filippo Tommaso Marinetti could all be seen at the Steins'; people such as Lytton Strachey, Bertrand Russell, Ford Madox Ford, Clive Bell, Duncan Grant, Roger Fry and George Moore 'turned up' from across the Channel. Marsden Hartley, Elie Nadelman, Alfred Maurer, Walter Pach and Maurice Sterne were among a permanent contingent of American artists. Guillaume Apollinaire was one of the main stars, a sort of master of ceremonies. He wrote a short tribute to the Stein *frères* (another of their nicknames), an elegant, whimsical doff of his cap to the siblings, whom he thought of erroneously as 'millionaires': 'Their bare feet shod in sandals Delphic / They raise to heaven their brows scientific'.[24] Their fame was fast growing, and these were self-consciously portentous times. Stein witnessed the celebrated performance of Igor Stravinsky's *The Rite of Spring*, where Vaslav Nijinsky's choreography caused riotous uproar (there she met Carl Van Vechten, the music critic for the *New York Times* who would become a lifelong friend); she lived among the crowd where Futurism, Orphism, Vorticism, Dadaism and modernism's many other -isms were to be born. A time of egoism and manifestos, and the context in which Stein eventually felt herself able to make her own grand, self-mythologizing, artistic statements.

Of course these meetings took place because of the paintings; the Steins would otherwise not have been at the centre of such an in-crowd. But once the Saturday evenings began, the personalities of the host and hostess became as much a draw as the art. Both were impossible to ignore. Leo with his nervous energy and his constant theorizing, Gertrude with her serene intelligence, a great listener, practically silent in these early days, apart from her well-known laugh (so hearty it was compared to 'a beefsteak'[25]). Alfred Stieglitz said he had never known anyone sit so long without talking. Her quietness may have been down to the fact that she was still learning French. Later she would fire unnerving questions at the guests. Vying with such a profusion of talented and vociferous men was a crucial part of her self-determination; it was no shrinking violet who would make her mark.

Stein's new, star-studded life as an accidental, if natural-born, Paris salonière contrasted sharply with her private life as a writer; here in the atelier on the rue de Fleurus the writing habits of a lifetime began, and her writing life, as her apartment filled with people, was necessarily solitary. An important condition of Stein's writing life in France was that it left her linguistically isolated. She relished the fact that the language surrounding her was not English; while the daily business of life might be conducted in French, she would not write in French until very late in her career, in 1938, her book *Picasso* being her first sustained effort to do so. It was an accident, not a planned manoeuvre, that she ended up in a place that gave her what she saw as this linguistic freedom, 'all alone with my English and myself ', as she wrote in *The Autobiography*.[26] Most of the people around her could not read what she wrote, but anyway at first they did not even know that she wrote.

She loved the perverse privacy of this double life, that nobody intruded on or made demands of her as a writer. She wrote through the night and went to bed at dawn. Hidden away upstairs she began writing in pencil in French children's schoolbooks of the kind she would use for the rest of her life. Here there was freedom from her teachers' sanctions about her style that had made her revise her work, and her famous refusal to edit began during the writing of *The Making of Americans* as she nurtured the belief, and later clung to it desperately, that the more she put into it the better, or truer, it would somehow be, willing it to become her magnum opus. Solitude, and deliberate artistic loneliness, imbue that book, and became its self-reflecting subject.

By 1906 Picasso had nearly completed his portrait of Stein, but he was dissatisfied with it and finding it hard to finish, so, as Stein put it, he 'painted out the whole head'.[27] Stein went off to Fiesole for the summer (where there was another colony of American writers and artists surrounding Bernard Berenson, the art critic). And then, after all that time spent gazing at her impressive and inscrutable face, Picasso completed her head without her. John Richardson, Picasso's biographer, calls Stein's head 'this little area of repaint that won Gertrude recognition as one of the most familiar twentieth-century icons'.[28] It is not her face. It is Picasso's idea of her face, made of his impressions of her as much as what she looked like: a mask, and one of her many masks.

When friends complained that Stein did not resemble the great, prismatic face and the huge androgynous body, the heaped flesh and folds of girth, Picasso's shrugged shoulder of an answer was simple: 'she will'.[29] Characteristically unperturbed by the fact that he had painted her portrait by removing her head, or decapitating her, Stein said of the portrait that it was more herself than she was, in a typically tricksy comment on identity. 'It is the only reproduction of me which is always I, for me', she wrote in *Picasso*.[30] Hers is a happy re-appropriation of her own image, because Picasso had created an image of her that would become famous on the other side of the Atlantic in her native country before she herself did. She loved it, and was often photographed with it. It became the first of the icons of her celebrity and as such it was priceless. He gave it to her, free of charge.

Stein is at her most Sphinx-like in this portrait, in which Picasso used a 'very small palette' of unbecoming brown and grey.[31] Picasso's Stein seems to be listening and confiding at the same time, or perhaps about to impart some insightful gem. It was the pose in which she might have sat with Picasso and discussed their future careers, their fantasies of triumphant future burglaries in which the intruder would make off with his pictures and her writing instead of money or silver. The art critic Roger Fry published the portrait in *The Burlington Magazine*, next to a portrait by Raphael, suggesting that both were of equal importance. What came after it was 'the heroic age of Cubism' (Max Jacob's phrase), on which Stein continued to dine out for the rest of her life.

This portrait would stay on Stein's walls for 40 years (surviving the German occupation during the Second World War), until she died. Then Alice Toklas was its guardian, until it was sent to the Metropolitan Museum of Art in New York, the first of Picasso's works to be acquired by that institution. Alice wrote about the day it was removed for shipping. Picasso came round and they mourned together over the loss of Gertrude and their youth. 'Neither you nor I will ever see it again', said Picasso.[32]

There is no doubt that during the painting of this portrait, particularly in the solution to the problem of her face, Picasso resolved issues that would lead him to the transition to Cubism. Perhaps talking to her also helped clarify his ideas, but her image certainly inspired him. Richardson reproduces a series of Gertrude Stein 'look-alikes' in Picasso's work from around this time, 1906.[33] No doubt intrigued by her lesbianism, he was depicting pairs of women who shared her robust frame. The nudes seem to be modelled on Stein, and the new kind of femininity which she seemed to represent. In 1906–7 Picasso was working on *Les Demoiselles d'Avignon*, which could be seen as the first Cubist painting, and the studies for which were acquired by Stein. His portrait of Gertrude Stein, a kind of rejoinder to Matisse's portrait of Madame Matisse (also on the Steins' walls), enabled a breakthrough in his style, which was one of the paths by which he recreated twentieth-century art. Indeed, her claims in *The Autobiography* were not so exaggerated after all.

Pablo Picasso, *Gertrude Stein*, 1906, oil on canvas.

Nevertheless Stein did not buy a Cubist painting until 1911, and it was according to Leo the first painting at the rue de Fleurus that she had been solely responsible for purchasing. Stein was not a connoisseur in the same way that her brother was. She liked things she could relate to herself and her work. She immediately grasped the ways in which Cubism unlocked the possibilities of expression and description that could also be applied to literature; she too was moving away from realistic copying from life and beginning to appreciate the interception of the artist's consciousness as the thing of major interest. From Picasso she said that she also learnt that true artistic creation was necessarily ugly.[34] It was up to the followers of greatness to make art beautiful. Like Picasso she became, according to her own natural leanings, an iconoclast. In the late 1930s, when she wrote *Picasso*, she saw him as an inventor, and by extension herself also, in the tradition of Edison and Ford. She linked herself with Picasso because his work was ugly but maybe he was a genius – and maybe she was too. Leo's adverse reaction to Cubism also spurred her into liking it; it was her reaction against him and his intellectual dominance. Also, Picasso appealed to her vanity. In 1912 he painted her calling card into *The Architect's Table* – a canny move in order to get her to buy it, at a time when her financial interest in his work was flagging. She then started buying more of his Cubist works, as well as those of Juan Gris, although it cannot be denied that the earlier Picassos, the Cézannes and the Matisses that Leo had first fostered and gone out of his way to get hold of were better works of art.[35]

Gertrude's art appreciation was more limited than her brother's, though she did make her own independent purchases as well as choosing them with him. It was not surprising that the first painting Marie Laurencin ever sold was to Gertrude Stein, considering that it was a portrait of the habitués of the Stein salon, which was why Stein wanted it: another prop for the reputation. Like salon ladies of old, who commissioned portraits of themselves by the members of their own circle, Stein gathered laurels and homages from all the young and talented people around her. But she was happy to leave the role of art critic to Leo, for the while to be touched with genius by association, spurred on by an image of herself eventually basking in the limelight of literary creation. The Picasso portrait was her talisman.

In *Picasso* Stein writes that everyone was 'disconcerted' by the things Picasso was creating; it was her ambition that she too would

The salon at 27 rue de Fleurus, *c.* 1912.

disconcert with what she had come up with during their months together. In 1906, after sitting for Picasso, Stein completed the stories she had been working on the previous winter, eventually published as *Three Lives*. These 'three lives' are three portraits, written while sitting underneath Cézanne's *Madame Cézanne with a Fan*, so the legend has it.[36]

The three stories of black and immigrant working women were to be the making of Stein's genuine reputation as a writer, and remained at its heart for many years. They are still the most widely taught of her works. *Three Lives* differs from what came after it in the Stein *oeuvre* because it is still fairly easy to gather its meaning in a traditional way; in other words, the story is still fairly straightforward. Nevertheless at the time it was seen as a bewildering breakthrough in style. It caused Israel Zangwill to lament: 'And I always thought she was such a healthy minded young woman, what a terrible blow this must be for her poor dear brother.'[37] He would not be the last to mourn for her sanity. Stein reported this story with relish, but throughout her career, while her experiments and involutions, repetitions and departures became ever more radical and braver, she remained adamant that the language she was using was transparent and easily understood.

Three Lives was really the last point at which Stein's writing touched the ground, or rather the moment it took flight. The use of immigrant speech patterns in the two flanking stories 'The Good Anna' and 'The Gentle Lena' made them remarkable, but 'Melanctha' was the story that broke the mould. This was the beginning of her lifelong struggle to represent consciousness in words, 'the problem', as Edmund Wilson put it in a 1929 review of Stein's *Useful Knowledge*, 'of language itself'.[38]

The book began as 'Three Histories', written at the instigation of Leo, who thought Stein might try her hand at translating Flaubert's *Trois Contes* to improve her French. Both this book and Cézanne's paintings used working-class subjects. In her notebooks, Stein admired Flaubert and Cézanne both for their emotional attachment to their means of expression rather than emotional investment in their characters or subjects. In looking at Cézanne's painting she understood that her version of realism need not be about verisimilitude, and that – although on the surface the subject of *Three Lives* seems to coincide with that of American literary naturalists such as Stephen Crane and Theodore Dreiser, or even that of Israel Zangwill – in fact she was not very interested in being a realistic novelist. She was more interested in revealing the way the mind worked.

Her 'realism', then, in *Three Lives*, was an attempt to get at an inner value, an inner reality. The spatial relationships between objects or people, as Leo had taught her, were paramount in Cézanne. The painting became a separate object, rather than a pretence to exact representation. So, 'Melanctha' is 'about' the way the characters move in relation to each other.[39] This painterly metaphor allowed her to step back and look at the language itself and make of it an object seen from various angles, allowed her to be analytical of language and description and dialogue as parts of a composition. Her implicit notion of making demands on the reader is partly down to Cézanne, as is her idea that each element of the composition is as important as the next.

The book's epigraph was a 'quotation' from the symbolist poet Jules Laforgue: 'donc je suis un malheureux et ce n'est ni ma faute ni celle de la vie' ('therefore, I am unhappy and this is neither my fault nor that of my life'), and it is infused with the melancholy that still possessed the young Stein. It is obsessed with failure, as all her writing was at the time. Its heroines – servants, downtrodden people – are all doomed not by great or tragic events, but by a sort of recognition of their own unimportance, a tacit fading away. 'Melanctha', though a particularly powerful tale of a strong, plucky, daring character weakened by life's ordinary attrition, is another melancholy story which ends in its heroine's abrupt death.

In Stein's own terms, 'Melanctha' challenged the 'nineteenth-century idea' of a beginning, a middle and an end, because the way of reading it must be different, must take in a different idea of time. It exists in a sort of suspended moment of perception, brought about by involution, stasis and reiteration; progress itself is challenged by her plotlessness. All Stein's work would be characterized by reflection, rather than action, by her brand of twentieth-century scepticism.

Richard Wright, author of the books *Native Son* and *Black Boy*, praised for their realistic telling of black life, later said that when he read 'Melanctha' he 'began to hear the speech of [his] grandmother, who spoke a deep, pure Negro dialect'.[40] The African American poet Claude McKay perceptively disagreed: 'I found nothing striking and informative about Negro life. Melanctha, the mulatress, might have been a Jewess.'[41]

Though it was seemingly a portrait of black life in America, Stein herself declared that *Three Lives* was not an American book, and that incidents in 'Melanctha' were based on Parisian scenes.[42] In fact this was another dissimulation. 'Melanctha' is partly a recasting of the lesbian story *QED*. Those elements of it that were 'inaccrochable' ('un-hangable' – like a risqué painting) – to use the word Stein used when criticizing one of Hemingway's sexually explicit early stories – could be hidden behind a black, heterosexual mask. 'Melanctha' contains a self-portrait; Gertrude Stein is the male character, Melanctha's lover, Jeff Campbell, the doctor.

Stein, the woman who would have numerous portraits made of her by some of the century's most illustrious artists, was in 1904 or 1905 the subject of a sketch by her brother Leo. Perhaps this was the first portrait ever made of her. Stein's comment when trying to decide if the picture that Leo had done looked like her or 'like a nigger', was that 'it certainly comes to the same thing'.[43] However racist the assumptions that went along with it, it was her identification with another culture that stood behind the displacement of the roles of Jewish middle-class lesbians onto the African American characters of 'Melanctha.' There was never any great understanding of African America on Stein's part, but there was an interest and attraction.

If in 'Melanctha' Stein is substituting 'negroes' for women, as might be inferred from the displacement of middle-class women's roles in *QED* onto the black characters of 'Melanctha', this suggests an interchangeableness in her concepts of ethnic and feminine roles that was common in the early works of psychology and characterology that she was reading. There is a connection between Stein's interest in the voices of the servant, the ethnic outsider and the woman, each of which could be seen by psychoanalytic theory of the time as interacting with the 'primitive'; they are also supposedly prone to styles of speech which encourage play of language. (Harking back to the primitive and the indulgence of childish play are two of the key terms of Freud's concept of creativity.)

Stein was capable of sweeping statements about her own Jewish race as well as others. One well-known autobiographical moment from *QED* is Stein's insistence on her own linguistic exuberance: 'I have the failing of my tribe. I believe in the sacred rites of conversation even when it is a monologue.'[44] Stein's use of the word 'tribe' here draws a fairly explicit link between the primitive and the creative, the same link found in contemporary psychoanalysis.[45] The Italian psychologist Cesare Lombroso, whose work Stein had been reading, specifically located a link between stereotypical ideas of Jews and women as excessively loquacious. Stein proudly owns up to this, though the compulsion to tell one's experiences is a common trait linking neurosis with creativity in psychoanalytical theory. Her conversational skill and her wordiness would be her ticket to genius, as she saw it. (Later, Stein would be lampooned for being both 'primitive' and 'childish'.)[46] Taking on the voice of the immigrant, in *Three Lives* and later in *The Making of Americans*, reinforced her own position as 'racial outsider'. To some extent it was her intention, in the manner of a sociologist, to study something strange to her – African America – in order to uncover her own strangeness. But as Michael North has argued, Stein's use of 'racial masquerade' was a way of extricating herself from the traditional bonds of language and syntax, of placing herself in a strange relation to their rules.[47] She needed to speak a language that was deliberately removed from, at odds with, the ordinary. She wrote of her own feeling of being 'misplaced', of being a 'stranger'. Gertrude Stein has been called the first important American Jewish writer. The ways in which this affected her use of language, the intelligibility of her 'dialect', as well as how she saw herself and wanted to present herself as an artist, are complex.

At the aural level, the pidgin English that Stein fell into in her correspondence and which filters into her published writing, as well as her use of questioning effects, the repetitive variations on a single word in order to interrogate its possible meanings, her incantatory, prayer-like repetitions, have deliberate nuances of American Jewish patois, rather than a specifically African American dialect. In a poem written in 1915, 'Yet Dish', her rendering of 'Yiddish', Stein conjured with ideas of her by then very alternative use of language and its relation to her racial origins. The use of the present participle at the end of *The Making of Americans* may be intended to emulate the speech patterns of German immigrants; the idiom of her German relatives when they spoke English was itself also based around the present participle.[48] Then there is the 'Old Testament' style that Stein explicitly urged as the necessary medium of experimental American writing, as she moved towards a definition of the Great American Novel.[49] These are some of the most important elements of which Stein's new style is composed. While at first the role – her own Jewishness, the use of an 'immigrant' voice or dialect – was explicit, later it became subsumed into Stein's idiolect. And later still she would be accused of covering up her Jewishness, of disowning it. But these issues played their part in shaping her abnormal syntax, as well as her unique indeterminacy of meaning.

Melanctha, whether or not her blackness is convincing, was an astonishing character for Stein to come up with at this time. A story about a black woman's sexuality was extremely subversive, even if it was self-published, and even if, as it did, it relied on terrible stereotypes and displayed a nonchalant racism and miscomprehension typical of its era. Melanctha is a seeker of knowledge, and Stein uses 'knowledge' in the Biblical sense. *Three Lives* is full of sexual euphemism: 'Melanctha Herbert always loved too hard and much too often.'[50] Euphemism also became an important element of Stein's obscure poetic play, a major prong of her style which began out of a certain privacy, a personal squeamishness and reluctance to openly broach such subjects, although she later ascribed it a reason as part of her style. (The chief motive behind Stein's vehement objection to Joyce's *Ulysses*, apart from personal jealousy, was an objection to its lewdness.) *Three Lives*, like QED, was concerned with constraining emotion rather than letting it run wild.

By 1908 Stein had begun hawking it around potential publishers, and finally paid for its publication herself in 1909. This first publication was a momentous step, and she began publicizing her book with vigour. Interestingly she sent it to W.E.B. Du Bois and Booker T. Washington, the two pre-eminent African American scholars of the day, among others. Stein's letters of the period show that she was reading Arnold Bennett, who had a similar 'artistic obsession with ordinaryness' to her own,[51] and whose *Anna of the Five Towns* (1902) and *The Old Wives' Tale* (1908) had established him in a realist tradition that was hardly challenging the precepts of genre. Of all the contemporary authors in England, she chose to send copies of *Three Lives* to Bennett, H. G. Wells, author at this time of several realistic middle-class novels (among many other things), George Bernard Shaw and John Galsworthy (whose *The Man of Property*, the first novel of what would become *The Forsyte Saga*, had appeared the year before): the 'four Olympians' of the contemporary English literary scene, as the friend she had asked to distribute the copies dubbed them.[52] Originally Stein aspired to the popularity that each of these writers had attained. There were no contemporary writers to whom she could look for a precedent in the experimental work she was doing; she was masterless. *Three Lives* was, at the time, a reasonable critical success. It hardly sold any copies, but it did give her a name, and it made her talked about in all the right places. William James, writing to her three months before he died, called it 'a fine new kind of realism'.[53] To Stein it was only the start of her stylistic revolution. Realism, to her, was as staid as any other literary cliché; what she was wanted to reproduce was reality.[54]

Encouraged by the talk, passively awaiting 'the daily miracle', she wrote reams. She later wrote that there were only a few human functions – such as talking, wandering around, driving, reading, writing – all of which she seemed to suggest she performed with a certain inner passivity – that did not make her 'nervous'. She was obsessively compiling her notes and diagrams on the character traits of visitors to the rue de Fleurus. In monastic garb, as if styling herself a twentieth-century Balzac, she wrote through the night as the household slept, at work on a warped *Comédie humaine*. The great nineteenth-century novel cycles and family chronicles all fed into the grand ambition of *The Making of Americans*. In her notebooks she compared herself with various great male chroniclers whom she saw as geniuses, including Balzac, Zola and Johnson. Stein's famous pronouncements about her own genius began secretively, tentatively in the notebooks for *The Making of Americans*: 'maleness that belongs to genius. Moi aussi perhaps.'

Four

She began at this time a long book which has not yet been published called 'THE MAKING OF AMERICANS BEING THE HIS-TORY OF A FAMILY'S PROGRESS'. She used this as a study of style. It is tremendously long and enormously interesting and out of it has sprung all modern writing.[1]

So wrote Gertrude Stein in 1922. The wildly intemperate, self-advertising voice of *The Autobiography of Alice B. Toklas* made an early appearance, ten years before that book was written, in Stein's autobiographical notes for *Geography and Plays*. In fact Stein had written the first conventional strains of what would become the great, monstrous anti-novel in 1903 and returned to it in 1906–8, when she wrote the first major chunk of it. Claims like these were self-defensive – by 1922 *The Making of Americans* had still not been published – but made Stein an easy target for parodists.

Stein called it 'the long book'. When it was finally published in 1925 one reviewer seemed hardly able to believe that it was 'seven and one half inches wide, nine and one half inches long, and four and one half inches thick!'[2] *The Making of Americans* is more than half a million words long, and took eight years to write. It has often been called unreadable, and reading it from cover to cover is a punishing experience. In the 1920s Stein acknowledged this in her adage that 'everyone should be reading at it or it'.

The book was completed in 1911, meaning that it comfortably pre-dated the publication of Joyce's *Dubliners*, Woolf's *The Voyage Out*, and Eliot's 'The Love Song of J. Alfred Prufrock', and was written an easy decade before those monuments of high literary modernism by the same writers: *Ulysses*, *Jacob's Room* and *The Waste Land*. It was published, though, for the first time, three years after them. That it remained unpublished until 1925 created an enigmatic gap in Stein's reputation. It cannot be said to have influenced the world until the 1920s, when its innovation as well as its social concerns and contexts had already become obsolete. Yet there were reasons why Stein considered it her own grandest single achievement.

The Making of Americans reflects the new social arrangements of its time, albeit obliquely. It is about the making of an American national character. Written at a time of growing American nationalism and interest in the idea of national literature, and epically conceived, although its epic possibilities are never fully confronted, it asks the same question that had been asked since Crèvecoeur's famous 'what is an American?' Just as the word 'making' in Stein's title has many meanings, so does the presumption of 'progress' in the subtitle, 'being the history of a family's progress'. Perhaps the use of the word 'progress' was intentionally ironic. The novel subverts the assumption of the deliberately blithe opening sentence of William Carlos Williams's 'satire on the novel form',[3] *The Great American Novel* (1924): 'If there is progress then there is a novel.' In particular, the progress of the woman, the Jew and the self-made genius in America represent Stein's own struggle to establish her artistic integrity in her first novel. In this 'making of Americans' Stein's image of America relies on contemporary nationalist feeling for the building of a new race;[4] the making of an American national character and an American national literature are linked. Stein was among the first of a wave of twentieth-century writers who were interested in remaking American identity in a country outside America. The tradition of Americans in Paris was illustrious, but yet to reach its full flowering, when after the war so many young men decided to stay on.

Radically ambitious, *The Making of Americans* resembles an autobiographical novel, a family saga and a modernist version of the *Künstlerroman*, but it was also conceived as a history, and evolves – or for some critics degenerates – into a complex study of psychological traits and typology. One reviewer, avoiding such distinctions, just referred to it as 'prose'.[5] The question of how *The Making of Americans* stands up to the terms of history, autobiography and scientific venture should be considered in the light of Stein's later flouting of genre (for example, her 'sonnets', which exhibit practically none of the traditional attributes of the sonnet), and transgression of discipline – literary 'portraiture' taken to extremes – as well as the upheaval in these classifications which was general to the period, but there remains the fact that during the writing of *The Making of Americans* Stein made the most important transition of her literary career. In writing it she began to realize that it was impossible to rely on sensory perceptions of the world around her, in the manner of most fiction writers. After it she would attempt to strip time and place completely from her work.

Just as her novella *Fernhurst* (1904–5) was set in a world where epigrams are exchanged over cups of tea, and the entanglements of QED (1903) were played out in drawing rooms, during museum visits and New York lunches and at the opera, *The Making of Americans* begins in a world of riding parties and marriage proposals, has its cast of low- and high-born characters, is on one level a generational family saga, and for the first 150 or so pages carries out its conventional scheme with perfect authorial tact.[6] The book demonstrates a nominal allegiance to the novel of sentiment understood as a feminine and bourgeois discourse. Stein was keen to belong to the bourgeois, but also to exist outside it, and she wanted to move beyond what she saw as a female literary idiom.[7] Following the final version's early 'magnificent' passages (Hemingway's term),

Stein was to decide that 'country house living' is 'an old story';[8] in other words, nineteenth-century class distinctions are broken down, along with the ways of representing them. 'I was trying to escape from the narrative of the nineteenth century into the actuality of the twentieth', she wrote.[9] Her ideas about individuality and equality found their way even into the grammar and punctuation.

The novel implicitly equates disruption of the rules of language with the disruption of social order. Stein pays minute attention to the small variations in the book's deliberately limited vocabulary. For example, the novel's superabundance of connective words suggests that the relationship between people can be represented by the relationship between words, as if trying to replace connections where they have been worn away by the world's changing view of history and family. Stein gave more importance to the little words – pronouns, conjunctions – and it is not hard to see the radical implications of the undermining of hierarchies by the disruption of word order. Stein's changing of conventional word order was intended to question the usefulness of such convention and order in describing the world. This was an almost anarchistic approach. It brims with oppositions and contradictions, irony, negative constructions and antimony, a way of building up ideas that would fascinate Stein throughout her career, and that would allow her a deep moral ambiguity in everything she wrote.

Stein's scientific training set her apart from the other creative artists in her milieu, and she traded on it. If, as Leo insisted, she was unable to express herself effectively in a traditional fictional idiom, she could shape her own that was infused with the language of science. Scientific practice being part of her approach, one of her aims was 'I want to be right about every one.'[10]

In order to be right she started generalizing with gerunds. She grouped people in their ways of loving, being, attacking, resisting and so on. She dropped punctuation, and sculpted massive paragraphs that got longer as the book went on, and sentences that

Stein in characteristic pose, 1905.

resembled scientific diagrams, categorizing human problems until
they were sufficiently abstract to be universal. She never revised,
on principle. The emphasis on the present, on observation, lies
behind the book's hubristic goal, to represent 'every kind of human
being that ever was or is or would be living'.[11] This modernist myth
of completeness that it chased was a way of drawing together all
the acknowledged disorder of her own mind.[12]

Stein was still abreast of developments in psychology, and in
1908 Leo had introduced her to a surprising source of encourage-
ment, Otto Weininger's *Sex and Character*. Although Weininger's

theories are now easily dismissed as absurd, he was once at the forefront of the burgeoning field of sexual theory. *Sex and Character* was first published in German in 1903, and Weininger killed himself the same year. The book ran into twenty-three English language editions between 1906 and 1927.[13] Stein first read it in 1908, before she read Freud and while she was struggling with and on the point of abandoning work on *The Making of Americans*.[14] It became a big influence on the novel.

The unsavouriness of Weininger's thesis – it expresses violent antipathy towards women and Jews[15] (though he himself was Jewish) – makes it hard to believe that Weininger was more of an influence on Stein than was Freud, but he was. Although Weininger's anti-feminist and anti-Semitic tirades make him an odd choice of model for a Jewish woman, his allure for Stein was based on his objection to heterosexual sex, his so-called 'liberal' attitude to homosexuality laws, his notion of the misunderstood genius and his suggestion that of all women, the most masculine are the most likely to be capable of an act of originality and creativity. Although she never espoused the overt race hatreds of the kind Weininger distilled, Stein's notebooks of the period show a disturbing vein of misogyny. Weininger's conception of the 'absolute female' as weak, stupid and vain, as lacking imagination or a genuine sense of beauty, seems to have spurred Stein further into seeking a masculine identity for herself.

Weininger's rejection of sexual dimorphism was appealing for Stein; he saw sexuality as a sliding scale. Feminist debate at the turn of the century also centred round the question of what masculinity and femininity were, in essence; 'The woman question' was a scientific as much as a social question. As early as 1894 Stein had shown an interest in male and female character formation in her college theme 'The Great Enigma', where couples are seen as 'antipodes'.[16] In *The Making of Americans* she used ambiguous terms like 'independent dependent' to replace traditional gender classification.

The correlation between body and mind, sex and character, allows Weininger to examine the whole organism through numerous physical analogies for mental processes. But Weininger's struggle was to prove or describe his contentions without resort to external phenomena. Stein also deliberates over the relation of perception to sensation, offering various ways of coming to terms with describing without sensation. In *Tender Buttons* this would reach its most radical point yet in her work, with the dissociation of words from their physical referents.

Infused with Weininger's influence Stein's book became an assortment of patterns, schemes, stylizations. The narrator attempts to describe kinds of people, and proportions of kinds in each person; levels of dependence and independence; each person also has a 'bottom nature' which reveals itself through repetitive actions. She so reduced things to their bare essentials that she ended up with contradictions, truisms, repetition and long, long, punctuationless sentences. In the final section no names or references to people are given; they are just referred to as 'some', 'any' or a 'kind'. While use of the pronoun 'one' rather than 'she' or 'he' was a strategy that allowed Stein to be drastically ambiguous about the gender of her characters, she was also toning down her truths until they become so mundane as to be worthy of the title of absolute certainties. Also they are so mundane that they can only have meaning as part of the whole, as words in a book. In a particular way they are empty of their individual meanings.

Weininger's double dream of a fully realized Kantian masculine identity inhabiting a world cleansed of all subjective demands, although extreme, had sources in many of the same anxieties which the most celebrated modernist writers faced, and it was fraught with the impossibilities of overcoming the eternally sensually contingent concepts of gender and ethnicity. Weininger has been seen as an emblem of the way early twentieth-century writers used scientific theories to help them represent the processes involved in the construction of identity. After Stein had finished with him, many male writers (among them James Joyce, D. H. Lawrence and Jack London) used his ideas to represent the difficult story of becoming a man in the modern world. Stein too had seen his book as a sort of parable of her own struggle to be a genius, for which she seemed to believe she had to rise above her own femininity and, to an extent, her own Jewishness. Stein was by no means self-hating, but she did see herself in a masculine role throughout her life, and as her drafts proceeded she removed all reference to the Jewishness of the characters in *The Making of Americans*, calling them instead 'middle class', the very epithet to which she clung in describing herself. Once again, she wanted to be normal, an every-man, while also wanting to be outstanding.

Stein cultivated an image of herself as a wholesome American, and many have noticed uneasily that this meant not talking about her Jewishness. She had to put up with casual anti-Semitism even from friends; she never celebrated her (non-practising) Jewishness, but, as she put it herself, she also 'never made any bones about it'. She was also a fierce American patriot. Her poem 'The Reverie of the Zionist' (1920) contains the lines:

> Don't talk about race. Race is disgusting if you don't love
> your
>   country.
> I don't want to go to Zion.
> This is an expression of Shem.[17]

This poem juggles with several confluent ideas about Judaism, stirring and meditating rather than reaching a final conclusion.[18] By 1928 she was apparently describing herself to a nephew as 'the most famous Jew in the world'.[19] But addressing a different audience in her autobiography four years later she commented that she didn't like the look of one of her guests; 'he looks like a

Jew', she tells her friend Alfred Maurer; 'he is worse than that', he replies.[20] She makes no mention of the fact that she herself is Jewish.

For Stein, being an American superseded any other allegiance, racial or cultural. Horace Kallen, the Jewish-American philosopher and pluralist, wrote in 1915 that people 'cannot change their grand-fathers'[21] – perhaps Stein 'assertively appropriates' this sort of terminology in the opening pages of *Making of Americans:* 'We need only realise our parents, remember our grandparents and know ourselves and our history is complete', she writes.[22] She liked being her own person, self-made: a genius sprung from nowhere. These concerns may also have influenced her decision to move away, in her writing, from sensual contingencies. What she liked about Oakland, California – and even more about Paris – was that nobody cared who your father was. But just as Kallen suggests that a person is nothing without his racial heritage – if you stop being a Jew, Pole or Anglo-Saxon you stop *being* – Stein seems to be asking, in her novel, what exactly is left without those relational identities. (She is asking, in other words, a very race-conscious question about American assimilation and pluralism, implying the 'race sui-cide' which she had written about in early compositions, including one called 'The modern Jew who has given up the faith of his fathers can reasonably and consistently believe in isolation'.)

Stein's audacious new style, then, was not as divorced from the social contexts of the long period over which it was written as has sometimes been supposed. The most radical changes in style came with her own half-fearful recognition of how far she had moved from presenting them in a traditional way. These changes were so important to all her subsequent writing that they warrant some explanation here.

Halfway through the novel, Stein decided to reuse her novella *Fernhurst*. Incorporation of the old novella into the new novel caused her to register the momentous change of style she was undertaking. The narrative breaks off and the subject turns to the narrator's own dissatisfaction with the emptiness of her former work, which she has been trying to convert into the new style. The narrator begins to discover mistakes in her own writing as she copies from one manuscript to another. She finds herself unable to trust the words she is using to convey her proper meaning; indeed, her former work seems to have lost all meaning. After faltering attempts to recommence in the new style, she begins to express deep despair about her own writing.[23] This is Stein's moment of authorial doubt made explicit.

This confrontation with the past in the form of her own writing fed into a self-consciousness about style and a revelry in self-doubt, played out within the pages of the book itself. Her anxious inability to copy correctly from her own manuscript led her to struggle with all notions of providing an accurate transcript of the past. The present participle clings to the present as the only possibility for certainty. Stein's narrator discovers that she can neither remember the emotion with which her words were once invested, nor recognize a manuscript in her own handwriting. What if one cannot be identified by a work in one's own hand? So significant is the act of writing in relation to personality that this spirals into a distrust of identity. By examining her former text, her former idiom, within her new one, Stein addresses the impossibility of knowing even one's own former self, let alone anyone else. Writing seemed to demonstrate that you can never really know or be with anyone, that there may be no final version of the text, of any 'character', or of oneself. It may never say the thing which its author desires it to say. As she questions the very process of assimilating past and present involved in reading, the narrator comes to confront any piece of writing as an object, and to wonder what existence or truth it may have on its own.

Her upsetting of the fictional applecart may be taken as the ultimate act of bad faith on the part of the author herself. The passage in which Stein copies out her old words is almost uncanny in its enactment of Barthes' definitions of *jouissance* and *plaisir du texte*, the 'state of loss' imposed as the writer confronts the breakdown, which 'brings to a crisis [the reader's] relation with language'.[24] In these circumstances she wonders what she herself, her own character, and her own identity as a writer, let alone the characters in her novel, may actually mean. She forces an encounter between her old story and her new way of telling it. By illuminating the clash so harshly Stein also deprives the reader of pleasure, and makes an elaborate point of doing so. After forcing the traditional mode onto the ears of her listeners to the point where she begins to lull them back into traditional expectations of a traditional romantic plot, she lurches back into what she sees as her more honest style, able to rely only on this 'continuous present': concentrating on 'writing as it was being written' as she described it in *Narration*.[25]

This was a turning point in her writing of the novel and of her entire writing career, as she confronted the significance of seeing a piece of one's own writing as an artefact, divorced from sensation, no longer belonging to oneself after the passage of time. The passage of time necessary for this realization to take place became shorter and shorter as eventually she achieved a distance from her own writing even as she wrote it. The consciousness of her own performance, and the authorial distraction from the act of narration, are quite clearly connected to the notion of distracted writing. That is not to say that she is unaware of what she is doing. Brought to crisis point by her unhappiness with the necessary distance which exists between a writer and his own composition, the only way to reconcile herself with the fact that her words exist outside herself is to insist on the notion of writing as pure behaviour.

She was making a transition to a new style that completely discarded realism and its romantic accoutrements. Imitation was no longer the point. *Three Lives* had given her a taste of what could be done if one did not have to aim at verisimilitude, what technical liberation it could mean for the writer. It is supposed to be about the making of the American nation, but the drama in *The Making of Americans* is one in the writer's own mind. It is about her memory. A conventional plot, by confirming its own predictions, offers the reader a sense of satisfaction. *The Making of Americans* does not conform to this contract between author and reader; it continually predicts and rarely fulfils; by page 620 the narrator is still making hollow promises about the future of the plot. It becomes impossible for the reader to hold in his or her mind the number of projected futures for the story. Stein's disruption of causality makes uncertainty about the future an explicit part of the reading of the novel, reinforcing the thematic uncertainty about what the future holds for Americans. Repetition, not progress, becomes the source of security.[26] The book became famous for the sheer bulk of its repetition; each repetition forces the reader into looking at the statement in a slightly different way. The bafflement, the nervousness of the narrator/author becomes the main subject of the book. For the first time Stein put the silent workings of the writerly mind on display. *The Making of Americans* becomes a search for completeness, of love, stories, of character and of the book itself, hurrying towards each moment of completion, and its own completion, but continually delaying itself. She is in it herself, and talks about her own suffering, despair, shame, melancholy, discouragement, uncertainty and 'queerness'. At one point the narrator herself breaks down in tears. But near the end she begins to believe herself 'a great author', at least somewhere inside.[27]

Writing was something Stein did at night-time and in the early hours, going to bed as it got light. She called it 'the daily miracle'; it became almost a spiritual act, involving meditation and lifting herself out of the world of passing time. Memory was not to be trusted. The future was unimaginable. 'The continuous present', which was to become a major stylistic implement, was her only refuge. Many years later she would say that as a writer 'you have to denude yourself of time . . . if time exists, your writing is ephemeral.'[28] All her changeability of mood is recorded in this novel, which was not written as an amusement, but as a painful necessity. In later years immediate description would be possible, but here she was still preoccupied with the problem of narrative, memory and the past and what it had to do with a person's character and how to represent it, and edging, despite the many false starts, towards a kind of clarity.

The Making of Americans is the work of solitude, addressed to 'this scribbled and lined and dirty paper that is really to be to me always my receiver'.[29] This egoistic interest in the workings of her own pen, her own mind, led her to stumble on a meta-fiction before any other writer was doing anything remotely as daring or strange. Aloneness and self-reliance, in the absence of secure knowledge, became for her a vital part of the author's state of mind. The cocoon in which she wrote gave her both the safety to experiment at will and the freedom from criticism that would have prevented the grandness of the failure of those experiments (if she had ever been one to take criticism on board).

Her refusal to revise her work had many of her friends tearing their hair out. H. P. Roché, one of the subjects Stein had used in the book (who Stein somewhat patronizingly labeled a 'general introducer' in *The Autobiography*, and who was later the author of that other iconic tale of Parisian bohemia, *Jules et Jim*), wrote to her in 1912: 'I start reading your style only when I feel very strong and want in a way to suffer.' His main problem was the bulk of the repetition: 'Why don't you finish, correct rewrite ten times the same chaotic material[?]' He was concerned for her:

> More and more your style gets solitary – the vision remains great, and the glory of some occasional pages. – Rhythm? Oh yes. But that sort of rhythm is intoxicating for you – it is something like masturbation . . . Quantity! Quantity! Is thy name woman?[30]

Stein imperiously told him he wouldn't have written such a letter to a man, and he was cowed. She was, she wrote to him, a true artist, and as such he ought to respect the inevitability of her art, determined as it was by her personality, just as any male artist's was.[31] Her reply was pertinent to much of the criticism her work received long after 1912. What was for a long time denied Stein was an awareness of her own effects, that hers were willed departures from 'normal' literature, that there was method in her 'madness'. She would be dismissed as a sort of one-woman lunatic fringe. Both intensely theoretical and intensely personal, *The Making of Americans* is a record of her own failures, but nevertheless a breathtaking departure for any writer, even for the writer of *Three Lives*. It is on the whole a very hopeful book, although a doomed one. It is a tremendous feat of stamina. As Stein remarked of Cézanne:

> When he could not make a thing, he turned aside from it and left it alone. He insisted on showing his inability; he exposed his failure to succeed; to show what he could not do, became an obsession with him.[32]

The final way in which this novel establishes itself as part of the new 'American' literature, in the sense of the 'pure' literature of which William Carlos Williams would write, is its gradual recognition of the fact that the only thing it embodies is itself. After it she made the writer's necessary alienation from her own words a deliberate part of her style. Writing was not simply the expression of one's thoughts but a way of understanding one's own thoughts and how they work, how oneself works.[33] From here she needed to move to a style that could better help her marshal the erratic, disparate perceptions of consciousness.

One day in 1911, Stein apparently came downstairs and said: 'I've killed him.'[34] By this melodramatic announcement she meant that she had put an end to the 'hero' of *The Making of Americans*, David Hersland. (The self-willed, autonomous, American character, who represents her own artistic development, is masculine.) Killing the hero was a significant moment in her steady move into abstraction.

In 1908 Stein had written the first of her abstract portraits in words. The idea appealed to her because it did not require the pretence of a story. A portrait is only a snapshot, only concerned with the moment it describes – not a narrative, a story or a history. Later Stein would talk about trying to capture 'a space in time filled with moving' in her work. Portraiture would remain a major concept in her writing right up until and including the *Autobiography*. Between 1908 and 1912 she wrote 25 portraits. The first one of an individual was 'Ada', which was about Alice Toklas, and the portrait 'Sacred Emily' is the first appearance of Stein's famous catchphrase: 'Rose is a rose is a rose is a rose'.

While she made her friends and acquaintances the objects of her study, she was herself a popular subject for portraits; as well as Picasso's, there was, in 1907, the portrait of Stein by Félix Vallotton, and in the same year she was sculpted by Elie Nadelman. Later she was also pleased when Alvin Langdon Coborn, a prominent American photographer, took her photograph for a collection on remarkable women. It was the first time a professional photographer had asked her to pose for him.[35] And she very much enjoyed posing.

Stein claimed to have an artist's eye but not his hand.[36] In summer 1909 she first saw a Cubist painting, and returned Picasso's compliment by writing a word portrait of him. She was seeing things in the same simultaneous, dynamic and contradictory way that she described as Picasso's vision in this portrait. Stein's word portraits of Matisse, Picasso and Isadora Duncan, among others, were attempts to render a subject while allowing the play of ideas and sensations around the writer also to enter the composition.

Félix Vallotton, *Gertrude Stein*, 1907, oil on canvas.

The thing that remains constant is Stein's – the artist's – vision (this was an idea Matisse had expounded).

This was the beginning of what is commonly seen as Stein's 'difficult' work. The short, assertive sentences Stein used here were incontrovertible, and therefore a form of defence against criticism, of which she was by this stage getting plenty from her brother Leo. There was a further rejection of emotion. Her practice is all about control, not lack of control, although fragmentation has replaced narrative. She was making her writing more and more precise by depriving things of their historical, literary or even syntactical context.

A writer surrounded by painters, it was easy for Stein to draw parallels between the two disciplines, and the 'scribbled and lined and dirty paper' that was a common medium. Picasso liked using paper in his collages, such as *Au Bon Marché* (1913), which coincided with Stein's portrait 'Flirting at the Bon Marché' (the Bon Marché was the department store where she loved to window-shop); he also used calligraphy. Seeing her writing as an object, like a painting, was an appealing idea; the surface of the words was becoming more important than their meaning. This technique was interestingly connected to but divergent from that used by Apollinaire and what would later be called 'concrete poetry'. Although she was using painterly metaphors and discussing the graphic elements of her work, her interest was in language and words, not in, for example, the visual impact of their arrangement on the page.[37] Her work received important recognition when Alfred Stieglitz, the young leading light of photography and rue de Fleurus regular, published her portraits side by side with Picasso's in his magazine *Camera Work* in 1912. Stieglitz also pollinated the flowers of New York society with news of Stein and her work.

As well as taking her cues from artistic methods, Stein's work in turn influenced the way painters thought about their work. There was a profusion of 'object portraits' in the art of the Stieglitz crowd who visited Stein's atelier in the 1910s and '20s, including Francis Picabia and Marcel Duchamp, in the form of collages of found objects, pieces of sculpture and portraits made up of typographic elements.[38] Marsden Hartley wrote about the influence she had on him, and Charles Demuth, the American painter, was inspired by Stein's word portraits to create a series of eight 'poster portraits' of his friends, based not on physical likenesses but images with which the painter associated them, including an homage to Stein entitled

'Love, Love, Love'. Stein wrote about Marsden Hartley in her play *IIIIIIIII*, which was circulated at Stieglitz's 291 gallery in New York when Hartley exhibited there in 1914. (One of the miniature 'portraits' of Hartley which the play contains reads, for example: 'Point, face, canvas, toy, struck off, sense or, weighcoach, soon beak on, so suck in, and an iron.'[39]) In 1916 Hartley produced *One Portrait of One Woman*, in which Stein is represented by a large flame or halo; several lesser halos or candles cluster around her hearth.[40] The young painters were fond of laying their tributes at Stein's feet (or in Picasso's case the reverse, as his *Homage to Gertrude* was intended for the ceiling above her bed).

This new kind of portraiture was the context in which Stein's 'portraits' existed – although she had begun writing them over a decade earlier. The words she used were also 'found objects', often obscure impressions of everyday life or snippets of conversation, taken from their ordinary surroundings or functions in order to create another reality. There are also collages and found objects in the work of Picasso, Juan Gris and Braque, all of whose work the Steins collected; for example, Picasso's *Still Life with Calling Card* and *The Architect's Table*, in which Picasso painted Stein's calling card into the composition.

By 1908 Stein had been at the point of rejecting realism. In 1912, still trying to expunge emotion and the problem of memory and association from her work, she moved from portraiture into still life, in *Tender Buttons*. She started writing 'plays'. (For her, calling something a 'play' was less to be constrained within the limits of genre suggested by that word than to suggest that she herself was at play when she wrote it.) Dialogue then began entering other pieces, not just the plays. She started incorporating overheard speech, and began using columns in her work. She wrote a piece called 'One Sentence', a misleading title for a piece that was thirty pages long (and not a sentence), and 'Storyette', a one-paragraph story. These were endlessly experimental years, and each new composition seemed to yield new methods. This was the most concentrated period of creativity in her life. It was a casting aside of literary decorum that coincided with her discovery of a new domestic arrangement.

She was becoming estranged from Leo. By the 1930s, offended by the offence he took at her work, Gertrude would deny his existence. When once she happened to see him in the street, she merely nodded, then went directly home and wrote a piece called 'She Bowed to Her Brother'. Already in 1910 another person had taken his place as the main influence in Stein's life. When she started writing she claimed that it was for 'myself and strangers'; now she was writing for somebody else, her perfect reader, Alice Toklas.

Five

Gertrude Stein and Alice Babette Toklas, the authors of their own great twentieth-century love story, found each other through an unwitting go-between. During the writing of *The Making of Americans*, while Stein was filling piles of notebooks with her analyses of friends and acquaintances, she pounced on Annette Rosenshine, a young woman with a hare lip, a cleft palate and a lack of social skills, who had travelled to Paris with Stein's brother Michael and his wife Sarah. Stein used Annette as a typist and errand-runner, but also as a guinea pig for her theories on character. Every afternoon at four o'clock the girl would submit to intrusive enquiries about all aspects of her personality out of devotion and a faith in Stein's ability somehow to cure her of her malaise, and the neuroses Stein had invented for her. She became one of her early disciples. She also let Stein peruse her personal correspondence. The letters from Annette's San Francisco friend Alice Toklas piqued Gertrude's interest. They told of Toklas's flirtations with other women, her bohemian life in San Francisco, her artistic interests, her sophistication and her certainty that coming to Europe would be the break for freedom that she needed. For nigh on a year Annette showed Alice's letters to Gertrude. So when, Alice barely having stepped off the boat, Stein and Toklas met in 1907 Stein already knew this strange fellow Californian who seemed half-bluestocking, half-gypsy. Stein, perhaps calculating the demeanour which would most attract Toklas, was immediately stern with her; Alice seemed to fall instantly for Gertrude. Annette fell out of favour, and Toklas replaced her as secretary. Soon she became a regular at the Saturday nights. They took long walks together in the Bois du Boulogne. Then when they took a holiday together in Fiesole in the summer of 1908, Gertrude made Alice a proposal, and Alice accepted.

Female marriage was not unheard of. There was a nineteenth-century precedent, particularly in 'bohemian' circles, which could sometimes also be recognized and accepted by wider society, and involved cohabitation, legal arrangements and one partner referring to the other as her wife.[1] By 1910 Toklas had moved in to 27 rue de Fleurus as Stein's wife. This turn of events probably led, indirectly, to the eventual departure of Leo from both the flat and the affections of his sister. But Stein's melancholy years were over. Her dependence on Alice in her life and work had begun. They would be together for another 36 years, until Stein's death. After that, Toklas devoted the rest of her life to polishing the public memory of Stein.

Mabel Dodge, the socialite, memoirist and early rival for Gertrude's affections, called Alice a 'hand-maiden',[2] but she was far more than that, and formidable. For Stein, Toklas was both an exotic and a familiar presence. In San Francisco Toklas had met, somewhat incongruously, Jack London, and been a sometime frequenter of the city's 'Bohemian Club'. She had an inner grit and a determination to liberate herself.[3] Her acerbic wit was well known, and of the pair she was often regarded as the better raconteuse.

The iconic pairing of Stein and Toklas as one of the twentieth century's most famous gay couples has meant a huge amount of discussion of the dynamics of Gertrude and Alice's relationship. Following Ernest Hemingway's sneaky revelations about the supposed overheard altercation between 'lovey' (Stein) and 'pussy' (Toklas), and its sadomasochistic hint (in his memoir *A Moveable Feast*), critics have speculated somewhat pruriently about the role

Alice B. Toklas and Gertrude Stein, 1922.

of each woman in the relationship. Alice has been characterized as everything from a shrew to a doormat. Despite the inevitable unearthings of evidence of rows and bickering, misunderstandings, jealousies and possible infidelities over the years, Alice's devotion to Gertrude was profound. Alice gave Gertrude every home comfort she needed and performed the roles of muse and amanuensis, lover, cook, editor and housekeeper. Gertrude's luxury depended on Alice's domestic devotion to her. They joked that Alice had to get everything ready before Stein emerged for the day because she couldn't stand to see work being done. There had to be someone to do the housework in order for Stein to get on with the job of 'being a genius'. Perhaps it is only the fact that Alice and Gertrude were both women that makes this seem remarkable. In some respects she carried out the duties of a servant; in others the discreet actions of a loving wife; sometimes she was Stein's agent. She was content to be named in public as her 'friend', or her 'secretary'. Many have suggested that Alice was the one who wielded power over Gertrude, who scolded and censured her, and chose with whom she could and could not be friends – that Alice, once crossed, was the real reason for magnanimous Gertrude's many fallings-out. In a suggestive example, when Annette Rosenshine came back to Paris and the rue de Fleurus in 1928 to proudly show Gertrude her sculptures (twenty years after they had been intimate), Alice steered her away, abruptly and silently turning out the lights, so that Gertrude could not even see them.

A large part of Stein's cultural significance as a gay icon is due to her 40-year monogamous relationship with Toklas, because it was both so groundbreaking and so obvious and unembarrassed. As Terry Castle has written:

> Stein and Toklas got people used to them and to the style of human intimacy they so vividly embodied. For half a century they acted as if nothing strange had happened and everyone who met them agreed that nothing had.[4]

(Although in the Paris they inhabited, behind their backs the details of everyone's sex lives were talking points for everyone else.) It is a glossy image of an idyll which may not quite do justice to some of the prejudice the couple faced, and faced down, but there is a truth to it. They had a lot of front, but also a lot of optimism. More often than the occasional sniping, they were respected and loved, as a couple, by an extraordinarily diverse group of friends. The fact was that their relationship was more secure than those of most of Stein's heterosexual Left Bank friends and contemporaries. Gertrude and Alice avoided being part of any lesbian clique in Paris; they did not cross-dress, nor were they melancholy misfits, nor did they fall in with the type of free-spirited Sapphic idealists epitomized by Natalie Clifford Barney and the frequenters of her 'temple of friendship'.[5] Although they were friends with Barney, and with Romaine Brooks and Radclyffe Hall, they had no interest in being part of a lesbian scene, and indeed were shocked by the behaviour of some of these groups of women.

Virgil Thomson recounted a catty story about Stein's lesbian 'credentials' within the Paris milieu. He once asked Stein and Toklas where Natalie Barney got her lovers from. Alice, who was 'always thinking the worst', said: 'I think from the toilets of the Louvre Department Store.' Gertrude was unconvinced, but her interest was piqued about who Natalie slept with. Out for a walk shortly afterwards, she bumped into a houseguest of Barney's, who she proceeded to grill about her hostess's sexual habits, in front of a crowd of people seated at the café Les Deux Magots. The guest went home and told Natalie about Gertrude's '*colossal* indiscretion'. Later, at a dinner party where various renowned lesbians were being discussed, when Gertrude and Alice were mentioned, Barney announced: 'Oh, nothing like that there at all. It's entirely innocent.' According to Virgil Thomson, this was Natalie's revenge: to make Stein seem like an ingénue, and make 'a fool of her in front of the lesbians'. [6] Unlike Natalie Barney, Stein would never rely on any scandalous image of herself as lesbian, or capitalize on it in any way. In the daily narrative that she wrote of their life, Alice is her wife, and she is Alice's husband, and that is how she saw herself.

When Stein wrote *The Autobiography of Alice B. Toklas*, in recreating the character of Alice, she seamlessly glossed over their living situation with the ladylike manners of Toklas herself; but simultaneously put it proudly on display for all to see, if they chose to look. The strategy has been alternately praised for its candour and noted for its 'deceitfulness'. But truth and deceit were uncommonly problematic concepts for Stein in the telling of her life, mainly because she was such a great manipulator of her own public image. Having created her persona, in the 1930s she made one for Alice, too. In the telling of the Rousseau banquet, for example, the detail of their hats was paramount – it was part of the joke, the character of Alice that she was interested in hats and food, like any good wife. In most of the photography they used to illustrate *The Autobiography of Alice B. Toklas*, they were conspicuously together, a couple. It was a normalization of their relationship that was unblinking and blatant, which makes it even more curious that it was bypassed by most people who read the book. The possibility that Stein and Toklas were lovers was apparently not even something to be considered by the American public when it was published in 1933; it simply fell beneath the radar of the vast majority of readers. And yet it was there, silently proffered without embarrassment, in photographic evidence. Stein would allow no intrusion beyond what she was willing to offer in this straightforward and unexplaining way. Offering this was in fact a way of saying that there was to be no further access. She repeatedly said that people could get any answers about her life from her work; she would have been appalled at the speculation about her private life which has flooded Stein criticism.

Although she saw herself as masculine, Stein did not cross-dress in the manner of such flamboyant Left Bank lesbians as Radclyffe Hall or the Marquise de Belboeuf. She did adopt a 'costume',[7] but her dress did not particularly mark out her sexual preference, as Ernest Hemingway's apparent innocence on that point during the early stages of their friendship would seem to illustrate. Despite her fairly masculine clothes Stein was not androgynous, and she never wore trousers. Her own idealized image of herself, in the character Adele in *QED*, was: 'large, abundant, full-busted and joyous'.[8] Although that largeness was a conspicuous element of her public image, she was actually quite small: five foot two inches in height. There were rumours (completely unfounded) of sexual liaisons with Picasso, and Alice was very jealous of her relationship with Hemingway. For him and for other male friends, Stein was confusing, in her kaftans and waistcoats, her monk-like robes. Stein sported a combination of brown velvet and corduroy suits and skirts, brocaded waistcoats, tweeds and a succession of roguish hats that was hard to locate culturally and worn with a style that would have been hard to emulate. (Later Stein and Toklas were dressed by Pierre Balmain, that byword for French sophistication in fashion, having befriended the young man. Attending the opening of his collection with Cecil Beaton after the Second World War, they agreed not to tell people they were wearing his clothes, in case they did the up-and-coming designer a disservice.)

Stein was charming and flirtatious, and enjoyed male attention. She liked being looked at, and relished clothes and accessories, hats and brooches in particular. What should she claim to have bought when her autobiography became a bestseller but 'the finest coat made to order by Hermès' – and a new collar for Basket, the poodle which was photographed almost as often as Alice, and a vital part of the Stein ménage in the public perception. (The Dutch painter Kristians Tonny even painted Basket's portrait. Basket was succeeded by another poodle called Basket ii. They also had an incestuously minded dog which they named Byron, given to them by Francis Picabia. Stein cast the light of celebrity even on the dogs around her – in one of her repetitive slogans: 'I am I because my little dog knows me', and in the statement that she liked to listen to her dog's lapping of his water to find the rhythm of a sentence.) Most male accounts of Stein see her as a comforting, motherly figure. It wasn't until 1927 that she cut her hair into the close crop that had by then become the fashion – unlike many of her contemporaries, until then she wore it long and lustrous, but usually piled up on top of her head as in Picasso's portrait. When she finally cut her hair, Picasso chastized her for ruining his portrait of her (one wonders if she felt a certain satisfaction in doing so), and Sherwood Anderson said it made her look like a monk – a remark which pleased her.

Beyond their public image, Stein's sexuality and her relationship with Alice had a profound effect on her work. In the early

Stein with dogs.

1910s Stein was still practically unpublished, aside from the self-published *Three Lives*. This, however, is one of Stein's most prolific and innovative periods. She produced her long novel, *The Making of Americans* (finished in 1911), numerous portraits and plays and her celebrated collection of poetry, *Tender Buttons* (1912, published 1914), among a host of other titles. In fact Stein was at the centre of the making of what we now see as the tradition of the avant garde. Much of this work pre-empts various aspects of literary modernism and postmodernism. It was as if her alternative lifestyle had freed her up to create alternative art. The two are intimately connected. The fact that she so ostentatiously proclaimed herself an artist and an avant-gardist – in her dress, her talk, her writing – also gave her the licence to live that alternative life without censure, exempted her from ordinary rules. This included producing an alternative to the masculine literary culture within which she worked, which became more deliberate and self-conscious as time went on, and her writing about women became more elaborate. Though she was capable of misogyny, Stein wrote about women all her life, and found them more interesting as subjects than men.

As she finished *The Making of Americans*, Stein was occupied with a number of other splinter projects. The titles of Stein's works of the period – as well as the portraits, between 1909 and 1912 she wrote *A Long Gay Book*, *Many Many Women* and *Two* (a portrait of herself and her brother) – suggest that she was considering her own individuality and uniqueness, her difference and abnormality, and her relation to others. 'The Making of an Author being a History of one woman and many others' was one proposed title for *Three Lives*.[9] During this period Stein was also at work on the long, experimental and radical *GMP* (Gertrude Matisse Picasso), designed as a sort of triptych linking herself, Matisse and Picasso.

Up until these works, she had written grammatically correct sentences, although her rhythms and repetitions had been unusual.[10] Here, however, she no longer felt obliged to do that. This is where the syntax itself began to break apart. So, for example, she felt able to write verbless sentences: 'A cushion, no fan and no rose, no cushion no fan no rose, no rose and no fan, no fan no cushion, no cushion no rose.'[11] She was now free even of the rules of syntax, for the first time. In an interview given years later she said 'words began to be for the first time more important than the sentence structure or the paragraphs.'[12] (Most of Stein's interviews and commentaries on her work are distantly retrospective, as she had only a very small readership until the 1930s.) Ironically *GMP*, in the very title of which she tried to promote herself as a contemporary and equal of Matisse and Picasso, was the piece in which she started to move beyond them, and art in general, as models for her writing. But the most surprising and bewildering changes were to come in the playfulness – including a new erotic mischief – of *Tender Buttons*.

The ways in which Stein's relationship with Alice affected her work can hardly be overestimated. As Shari Benstock pointed out in her groundbreaking study *Women of the Left Bank*, after Alice Toklas moved in to the rue de Fleurus in 1910, 'the elements of the living situation became subjects of virtually all of Gertrude Stein's writing, not only all her openly erotic poetry – but many of the ensuing word portraits and meditations.'[13] It was love, and after love her writing became 'joyful and capricious' in a way that it had never been before. They holidayed in Tuscany, Spain, Italy and Tangier, enjoying a romantic life together that was accompanied with lots of working. While waiting for the miracles, Stein filled mountains of notebooks with events, non-events, contentments, details, doubts, experimenting with new ways of putting words together. The domestic haven of their relationship gave her the stability that she needed, and their love, sexual, comfortable, petulant, sometimes jealous, day to day, was what furnished her 'subject matter', to use the term loosely.

The portrait 'Ada' (1910) is Alice's first entrance into the writings, although she also appears in *A Long Gay Book* (1909–10). She brought a new, poetical dimension to Stein's writing. Until Stein met Alice, she was going through a series of avatars: Hortense Sanger in the early compositions; Martha Hersland in *The Making of Americans*; in her early notes for *Three Lives*, there was to be an authorial narrator called Jane Sands. (Stein was a fan of George Sand – probably she also liked the coincidence of their initials.) But when Alice arrived, she stepped into the role of alter ego. The troubled Stein found in Alice the reader, the character and the answering voice she had coveted.

Alice had worked on the proofs of *Three Lives*, then typing up *The Making of Americans*. Then when Gertrude asked her to move in with her and Leo, she became a general factotum. As such she had hands-on involvement in the drafting and typing out of the manuscripts; she would query points in the margins, and this shifted into sometimes quite fierce editing. When she was preparing the manuscript of *The Autobiography of Alice B.*

Toklas (in 1932), written by Gertrude but appearing nominally in her own voice, Alice came across a passage in which Gertrude wrote that Alice had unflaggingly typed out every word of *The Making of Americans*. She vehemently deleted the second part of the sentence in which Gertrude had made her say: 'and I enjoyed every minute of it'.

Living with Alice gave Stein the worldliness she longed for, and the security. Her love reciprocated and a new confidence found, with Alice she truly became Gertrude Stein. The work changed too. After *The Making of Americans*, there is an evolution towards the esoteric style that Stein was famous for, what the papers called 'Steinese'. It became more discursive, less categorical. Paragraphs were abolished, and narrative was out the window. A new gamesomeness infused the work, and meaning, rather than being battened down, began to slip in and out of view. Her mature style was taking shape.

The explanation for the transition from sadness in QED, *Three Lives* and *The Making of Americans* to ebullience and confidence in *Tender Buttons* and the poetical works that followed lay with Alice. After 1910 Gertrude's work became full of Alice. Her writing about Alice is tender and thoughtful and philosophical.

A Long Gay Book contains this shift. It begins in the plodding methodology of *The Making of Americans* and bursts into poetry,[14] as she conjugates words and conjures with syntax, rhythm, the look of words on the page. Their senses splinter, re-intertwine and fall apart again. They elongate into columns. They sputter into abrupt, morse code-like admonitions: 'Notes. Notes change hay, change hey day. Notes change a least apt apple, apt hill, all hill, a screen table, sofa, Sophia.'[15] She puns, uses half-rhyme, homonyms and near-homonyms, edging outwards from intelligibility into some other work of consciousness, imaginatively questioning the meanings of words. She moves from exactness to open-endedness:

A lake particular salad.

Wet cress has points in a plant when new sand is a particular.

Frank, Frank quay.

Set of keys was, was.

Lead kind in soap, lead kind in soap sew up. Lead kind in so up. Lead kind in so up.

Leaves a mass, so mean. No shows. Leaves a mass cool will. Leaves a mass puddle.

Etching. Etching a chief, none plush.[16]

In *A Long Gay Book* Stein is in love: so obsessed with couples and coupling that she wants to pair up 'everybody I can think of ever'.[17] In it she seemed to recognize that this is a new start. As it concludes there is the joint soberness and exuberance of the line: 'All I say is begin.'[18] In it Stein has given in to non sequitur and lyrical patterning; gone are the diagrams and lists; she is alive again to beauty in a way that she had not been since her college compositions. Her apparent docility was changing into assurance – even if it did mean taking on a masculine role. On the other hand, she was moving into a world of subjectivity and ambiguity, and this, if one were to take a feminist-deconstructionist point of view about it, could be connected to the fact that she was also writing more and more about women. Alice was a mistress and a muse. She became a presence, an addressee and a questioning voice in the work.

Over the years *Tender Buttons* has been seen to require an extraordinary amount of explication for such a short text. The idea behind it was that her literary portraits had become too difficult because, being of people, they necessarily involved memory and storytelling of a sort, however abstracted. So she began this book of still lifes as an attempt to render the visual perception and the experience of each of these commonplace things: objects, food and rooms. As with Picasso's use of found objects in his still lifes, Stein removed words from ordinary usage and allusiveness, showing the way in which words become overused props – or rather preventing the reader from unthinkingly relating them to their usual associations. For example, the whole of the piece called 'Dining' (a favourite of Jean Cocteau's) reads: 'Dining is west.'

Tender Buttons was a transitional work, releasing Stein into compositions in which she could be without a plot or direction, amoral, idle, contemplative, evasive and untrustworthy, in which nouns were not even a way of naming things. It was an indirect, implicitly transgressive discourse that gave the parts of speech that were normally ignored more prominence. In the lecture 'Poetry and Grammar' she called it her *Leaves of Grass*.

One critic said it was like having an egg beater applied to his brain. But the urge to decode it all, to find answers, as if the pieces are riddles, is misleading. Deliberately elliptical, never conclusive, it is designed not to be 'understood' in the traditional sense. This is the most radical aspect of Stein's radical work. In the 'Food' section, in a piece called 'Orange In' when she wrote: 'real is, real is only, only excreate, only excreate a no since',[19] she was punning on the words 'realize' and 'realism'. What is real? What is created /excreted, and what is nonsense? And who is the judge of this? When contemporary critics called it 'nonsense', because it could not be understood, they were unaware that this was her point. Rather than a single truth, there must now be a variety of subjective truths.

In the final section of *Tender Buttons*, 'Rooms', she asks: 'does silence choke speech or does it not[?]'. Stein begins to play with the uses of the word 'lying' – not telling the truth and lying down (with Toklas), and 'giving it away' – or letting the truth be known:

Lying in a conundrum, lying so makes the springs restless, lying so is a reduction, not lying so is arrangeable.

Releasing the oldest auction that is the pleasing same still renewing.

Giving it away. Not giving it away, is there any difference. Giving it away. Not giving it away.

Almost very likely there is no seduction, almost very likely there is no stream, certainly very likely the height is penetrated, certainly certainly the target is cleaned. Come to sit, come to refuse, come to surround, some slowly and age is not lessening ... No breath is shadowed, no breath is painstaking and yet certainly what could be the use of paper, paper shows no disorder, it shows no desertion.[20]

The edges of silence, and what elements of seduction and lying can be put on paper, are addressed in a lyrical, open-ended, non-literal diction that becomes part of the dissimulation it describes; it becomes a way round the 'silence' that can 'choke speech'. But – for instance in the chiming of the words 'reduction' and 'seduction' – it also seems to ask what is lost as well as what could be gained by making the erotic life public.

From the hints at her erotic life in the book, it has now become a critical commonplace to say that the evasiveness of its style, coupled with its effusiveness, seems to have been born partly out of a desire to cover up and encode her relationship with Toklas. It was the beginning of a fascination with obliqueness to which she would ascribe various artistic reasons, but it began perhaps as a strategic dissimulation, a concealment: and yet it gave her the key with which to enter another literary space in which she could write to her heart's content about her love for another woman.

After the long gestation of *The Making of Americans* – she referred to it as a 'difficult birthing' – she had come to terms with one of her most enduring subjects: her own style. And her style was like nobody else's. It is a style that embraces tautologies and koans as the route to understanding in a way that plot and narrative, character, allusiveness, myth or just plain story could not do for Stein. The realization had come that she wasn't about reaching verdicts or definitive answers. She was a mistress of a fine anecdote, but her true work, that closest to her heart, could not have been a more intricate and ardent rejection of that as the basis for literature.

Her detractors were partly right in calling her a mystical writer – she did have a mystical sense of the power of words – she had a fanciful wish, in *Tender Buttons*, to create the whole world in its present moment as Shakespeare had created the Forest of Arden: without ever describing it directly. But she was a scientist too, and rejected sentiment. Stein's preference was to use a straitened, constrained vocabulary (the actual words of which, the limits of which, changed through phases in her career) in order to show up what goes on between words, among words, as the words are read and as they reach us as readers.

When she finished *Tender Buttons* she understood that it was a strange new beast. Finding a publisher for it was, then, a coup. It came about via a colleague of Carl Van Vechten's at the *New York Times*, who had launched the small Claire Marie Press, dedicated to avant-garde literature. A thousand copies were printed in June 1914. A less auspicious moment to be published could hardly be imagined.

Tender Buttons was met with bafflement far and wide. One reviewer summed up the general response by saying that Stein was 'either a colossal charlatan or mad'.[21] She was seen as Futurist, Cubist, anarchist. But it did also give her a serious reputation among the cognoscenti. Its importance was heightened in America, where the 'avant-garde' literature being produced in French in Paris was scarcely available, and *Tender Buttons* gained a small, devoted following for Stein. Nothing comparable had yet reached America. For many readers, it was the first encounter with such radical uses of the written word. Many who later wrote about its effect on them remembered that it had changed, or 'blown apart' the way they looked at words. Sherwood Anderson said it made him fall in love with words.[22] (That said, he was also a little in love with Gertrude Stein.)

The force of her American reception also had another out-come. With *Tender Buttons*, according to Stein, the papers began their 'long campaign of ridicule' against her.[23] Though it still smarted twenty years later, she did not want to paint herself as too grand to laugh at their jokes. When they parodied her, she asked them to print her work instead, because she was funnier than her parodists. Indeed there is humour in works like *Tender Buttons* and *Lifting Belly*, of a playful, convivial, teasing sort, an enjoyment in the non-literal resonances of putting words together strangely, in the open-endedness and indeterminacy of life. She could also be sharply witty in the naming of her pieces. When she offered T. S. Eliot *The Making of Americans* for publication in *The Criterion* and he tersely and evasively suggested he would need something more recent from her, she went home and wrote a piece whose title was 'A Description of the Fifteenth of November', the date they had met.

Tender Buttons (1912, published 1914) gave rise to a slew of other works including 'No, One Sentence' (1914), 'Possessive Case' (1915), and 'Lifting Belly' (1915–17), in which snippets of domestic conver-sation, endearments and chastisements showed that her works were no longer soliloquies, but addressed to Alice. From this point on Stein begins to speak to a lover in her writing, and there are often two voices to be heard in her work now – one pleading, one commanding, though the conversation (as Richard Bridgman pointed out in his seminal study *Gertrude Stein in Pieces*, the work begins to sound like a secret recording of a conversation) stops short of being sadomasochistic, as it has sometimes been called. The colloquies with Alice sometimes appeared in Alice's own hand, and there is some question about whether the two women were carrying on a real conversation, or a sort of collaboration.[24] Later, in 1932, Alice began writing more extensively in the manuscripts.

Throughout these works Stein was investigating, still, the gap between consciousness and writing. The decade between 1912 and

1922 was the period in which she gave fullest expression to her theory of the 'continuous present', in works such as 'Bee Time Vine', 'Pink Melon Joy', 'Possessive Case' and 'Lifting Belly'. Many of these works were not published in her lifetime. They are erotic pieces. Still more extreme in their dissociations than *Tender Buttons*, they are filled with private jokes, baby-talk, and pillow-talk. 'Kiss my lips. She did./ Kiss my lips again she did. / Kiss my lips over and over and over again she did.'[25] Echoing through the words are the moments of their life together: personal references that would not and could not be intelligible to others, which is what gave her work its famed sibylline quality. Stein brings the detail of Alice's life – cooking and cleaning – from insignificance into significance by enshrining it as literature, by calling it that. Unlike her masculine modernist contemporaries, Stein gave domestic themes a central place in the vast majority of her writing, up until and including her war writing.

Questions of self-censorship arise in relation to Stein's erotic work, which is the most stylized of all her work. When the sentence 'This must not be put in a book'[26] occurs in 'Bonne Annee', it seems to be a plea from Alice about leaving some parts of their private life beyond the putting of them into words. Stein was always courting Alice's approval in her work, and *Many Many Women*, for example, is stunning in its resistance to readability. Is the opacity related to hiding her relationship with Alice? Was her obscurity part of a disguise? Or was the erotic element of her work simply one strand of her enjoyment of a secret richness in words? The old idea that Stein disguised her lesbianism with linguistic play has given way to the idea that she was revelling in it.

In some ways Stein was surprisingly open about her sexuality, and some of the work is a celebration of gayness. In much of Stein's work gender is often random, ambiguous or interchangeable,[27] and her use of the word 'queer' or 'queerness' in *The Making of Americans*, as well as her use of the word 'gay' in *A*

Long Gay Book and 'Miss Furr and Miss Skeene' (1911, a portrait of two American painters of her acquaintance who were lesbian lovers) was provocative:

> To be regularly gay was to do every day the gay thing that they did every day. To be regularly gay was to end every day at the same time after they had been regularly gay. They were regularly gay. They were gay every day. They ended every day in the same way, at the same time, and they had been every day regularly gay.[28]

The word 'gay' in 1911 was not yet generally familiar as a synonym for 'homosexual'. However, by the time the piece was published in *Vanity Fair* in 1923, after which it became famous, Stein's insistence on the 'regularity' of the couple's 'gayness' could be said to be even more explosively loaded. But then again she could also be surprisingly coy. In *The Making of Americans* intimate or sexual details are skewed, hidden, locked away. While some women of her era were coming out in print, Stein trod a thin line of discretion.

Surely these new techniques were more than strategies of concealment. When she fell in love with Alice she had found an exciting new subject but she knew she couldn't really write about it – *QED* had been unpublishable, *inaccrochable*. But *QED* had also been an artistic failure – *Tender Buttons* was a crucial work because it released her into another world where she could write about these experiences, lovingly, poetically, philosophically, sophisticatedly. And in works like 'Lifting Belly' she was anything but coy.

Stein's sexuality was connected to her developing style in a complicated way. While not as simple as a lesbian code, Stein used certain words (such as 'Caesar', with its implied homonym 'seize her') in order to broach erotic subjects. 'Ada' was Stein's name for Toklas in her writing. She uses rhythm and acoustic effects like this: 'Aider, why aider why whow, whow stop touch, aider whow, aider stop . . .'.[29] In so doing she connects verbal trickiness, puns and euphemisms, the illicit or deceptive side of grammar, with the erotic life itself. That was partly because these were love offerings, and perhaps being 'put in a book' was never of paramount or primary importance. In 'Lifting Belly' she asks 'Can you read my print[?]'.[30] Though apparently intended for publication (Stein considered everything she wrote important enough for publication – and even wanted her receipts and shopping lists to be hoarded by the archive at Yale when she deposited her papers there), they were sufficiently obscure not to arouse unwelcome intrusion into the details of their life. Or so she thought. Since her death, critics have seized on them precisely because they do seem to offer a cipher that, if only it could be broken, would provide a way of probing and interpreting the true dynamics of the Stein/Toklas relationship. By 1925 the erotic strain in her writing would run its course, and so too would this element of her style.

Stein's 'double life' was more pronounced than others because she was 'toiling in obscurity' at the same time as basking in (minor) celebrity. Her work had so far gained little purchase on literary markets or the literary mainstream; she had miscellaneous pieces published in little magazines; people knew she was writing, but true champions of her writing were few, and those she had were ineffectual; publishers gulped at the unmarketable prospect her work represented. Leo was famously dismissive, which added to the developing rift between them.

By Spring 1913 'the old life was over'.[31] Leo moved out, taking half the collection with him, but leaving the Picassos. When Leo left Gertrude had been living with him on and off for the best part of 40 years. The break-up, and the break-up of the gallery, made the *New York Sun*. As Leo moved to Florence, Picasso and others of the old crowd moved to the suburbs. By 1913 the salon no longer existed in the same way as it had in those first extraordinary years. By 1910 Leo had stopped coming and Gertrude had taken the helm. Society hostesses such as Lady Ottoline Morrell now came to see her in Paris, along with artists such as Augustus John, Jacob Epstein, Marcel Duchamp and American painters Max Weber, Joseph Stella and Charles Demuth. Wyndham Lewis came, and *BLAST* solicited a contribution from her. 'The futurists are in town', she wrote excitedly in 1913, as if the circus had arrived.[32] 'They have a catalogue that has a fiery introduction demolishing the old salons.' Theirs was an iconoclasm of which she approved (though she would later denounce the Futurist worldview). 'After all we are all modern', she concluded her letter – there is a palpable sense of her delight at being part of a movement, the movement that would become known as modernism.

Leo's departure coincided with the first flowering of her international fame. It was in 1913 that US interest in Stein was roused by the ministrations of her well-connected socialite friend Mabel Dodge, whom she had met in Italy and about whom she had written 'The Portrait of Mabel Dodge at the Villa Curonia'. Dodge was as much of an instinctive self-publicist as Stein was, and saw to it that the portrait bearing her name was distributed during the hugely publicized event that was the Armory Show, a month-long exhibition of modern art in New York, including Duchamp's *Nude Descending a Staircase*. The Steins had lent Matisse's *Blue Nude* to the show, which became a *succès de scandale*; a copy of it was burnt along with an effigy of Matisse. Gertrude Stein was associated with this scandal, when the reprinted 'Portrait of Mabel Dodge', along with an essay on Stein by Dodge, hit the headlines. The papers were agog with the outlandishness of both the words and the images associated with Stein. This was her first big publicity coup. The *Chicago Tribune* poked fun at the Stein mystique:

I called the Canvas Cow with Cud
And hung it on the line,
Altho' to me 'twas vague as mud,
'Twas clear to Gertrude Stein.[33]

'Hurrah for gloire', cried Stein.[34] There was something innocent about Stein's instinct for fame. There was nothing cynical about it. Throughout her life she would rely on various unpaid propagandists (Dodge, Van Vechten, Sitwell, Hemingway, Alice) who were willing to put themselves out in her service, out of personal loyalty. The 'Portrait of Mabel Dodge' was also circulating in London. Throughout 1913, Stein was to be fêted as one of the most important exponents of the international avant garde.

More and more Stein was dependent on Alice's approval, and bowed to her in all questions of how to proceed with her work and her life. In 1913, at Alice's instigation, she went to London to find a publisher for *Tender Buttons*. There she met up with Roger Fry and other members of the Bloomsbury set including Virginia Woolf and Lytton Strachey. Her international fame was growing, but the international situation was to curtail its flowering at just that point. *Tender Buttons* was published in 1914, and war broke out while Gertrude and Alice were in London. 'It was a strange winter . . . nothing and everything happened.'[35] In March 1915 Gertrude and Alice went to Mallorca, fleeing the war and their fearfulness. They were to stay there for a year. During this year in Mallorca Gertrude continued to write her love epistles to Alice, as a sort of staving off of the horror. And it proved a year of bonding, and settling into the roles that each would live in for the rest of their life together. A year later, in March 1917 they set off in the Ford car they had shipped in from the US, in service of the American Fund for French Wounded, delivering supplies to hospitals. They had sold their last Matisse – the famous *Femme au Chapeau* – to fund their war work.[36] After the war, in 1922, they were both awarded the Reconnaissance Française.

Post-war Paris would never be the same, and the world of their salon was gone as they knew it. Apollinaire, the poet raconteur, would die in the 1918 flu epidemic; Leo had left and they would hardly speak again. After the war Paris would be filled with expats;

Working for the American Fund for French Wounded.

their little world was broken, their golden age gone. This golden age seems in the collective memory to have lasted for a generation, but in fact the events that made her a symbol of bohemia, and that were characterized and embellished in *The Autobiography of Alice B. Toklas*, the salon itself in this first incarnation, existed only between 1906 and 1913. In 1913 Marsden Hartley was writing to Gertrude somewhat obsequiously, as young men tended to write to her, that 27 rue de Fleurus was 'a place where genuine ideas thrive and mediocrity walks away with discretion'.[37] Here were the seeds of myth, the making of legendary stories. It was what brought American visitors of literary and artistic ambition in their droves after the war: the 'heroic age of Cubism' and of 'The Legend of Gertrude Stein'.[38] Yet it only lasted for a few short, resourceful years. Was it her, or her satellites; her, or her position of being able to comment on those around her that made this reputation? This was a question she would torment herself with: was it me or was it my work?

Stein would not be back permanently at the rue de Fleurus until 1919. Then it would be a different kind of salon, and she would be considered the old guard. Stein was nearing forty, and she had thousands upon thousands of pages of work that was still unpublished. She was 'dead broke'.[39] But during the war years Stein had been strengthened in all her artistic convictions, as well as in her personal life. She had been published sporadically and occasionally in *Life*, *Vanity Fair* and a number of little magazines. She had finally come into her own, away from Leo, and with Alice at her side. After the First World War, Stein was already a cult figure, and her star was once again rising, though in a different orbit.

Six

Stein's working life consisted of extremes of sociability and solitude. What she did almost in her spare time, the time off from writing, came to constitute a major part of her cultural legacy. Stein's own image for her salon, as refracted through the Alice Toklas narrator in *The Autobiography of Alice B. Toklas*, was: 'like a kaleidoscope slowly turning'.[1] What this suggested was that as the years rolled by an astonishing number of bright colourful presences came and went, the dynamics shifted, but all the time there was a focal centre: Stein herself.

By writing about it she cultivated the myth of her embodiment of Left Bank bohemia, but as the lives of 'heroic dissipation' that went on around her became more and more well known, she became more famous for her friendships with the great than for her own work. The salon was instrumental both in building up her fame and in obscuring her literary reputation, and for years afterwards she was known for genius by association.

The litany of famous names she drops in the autobiographies and who stepped through her atelier door includes William Carlos Williams, John Dos Passos, Djuna Barnes, Mina Loy, H. D., Bryher, Wallace Stevens, Salvador Dalí, George Antheil, Jacques Lipchitz, Lincoln Steffens, John Reed, Jean Cocteau, René Crevel, Tristan Tzara, Ernest Hemingway, Sherwood Anderson, F. Scott Fitzgerald, Paul Robeson, Erik Satie, Archibald Macleish, Josephine Baker, Hart Crane, Robert Graves, Laura Riding, Katherine Anne Porter,

Ezra Pound, T. S. Eliot, Nella Larsen, Paul Bowles and Aaron Copeland. Stein kept herself permanently in vogue via the perennial rejuvenation of having young admirers and followers.

That she managed to be both the centre of the most famous salon in Paris and a writer of such stature was unprecedented. No other salonière ever achieved in her own work the sort of influence that Stein would have over the literature of her time through her own writing. It suggests an extraordinary dynamism on Stein's part. But she was so successful as a hostess, and her writing was so audaciously different from anything else being produced, that at the time her writing was seen by the public as merely the by-product of her persona, or even a joke. When in 1923 Carl Van Vechten, writing for the *New York Tribune*, was able to say: 'Probably few writers are better known in this country than the American Gertrude Stein',[2] he meant that she, not her work, was phenomenally well known.

All the more extraordinary is Stein's rise to such a position in Paris of all places, where she was considered distinctly déclassé by traditional salon society. Salons had been authorities on taste and fashion in the arts and beyond since their heyday in the seventeenth and eighteenth centuries. By the end of the nineteenth century the salon was a very different entity, but it was still a cultural institution.

The stereotypical image of a salon hostess suggests a glamorous, moneyed, fashionable, perhaps personally under-talented woman, encouraging the male artists around her. Stein was not that rich, nor glamorous in any traditional way; she was a rough and ready, middle-class Californian. There was not much she had in common with her forebears of the *ancien régime* like Madame de Staël, or with Madame Récamier (about whom Stein wrote a play in 1930),[3] nor even, more recently, with Madame Arman de Caillavet, at whose salon Anatole France presided, or the Jewish salonière Geneviève Straus, on whom Marcel Proust's Duchess of Guermantes was based – or any of the *femmes savantes* of French literary and artistic history whose role was to facilitate and encourage conversation and intellectual exchange between the mainly male luminaries they surrounded themselves with. Regular meetings of salons would allow these literary and artistic lions to display their social standing. The old-style salon, as much as being a cultural meeting place, was an introduction to Parisian society, and a genteel preserve. This was how salons had always worked; one built a salon by positing oneself as the elite, and the arbiter of the elite, but one had to be part of that closed world in order to do so. The salon was an institution, and as such was ready to be demolished. The modern iconoclasts frequenting the rue de Fleurus were champing at the bit to break down the old salon culture.

When Gertrude and Leo came to Paris very few of the expatriate Americans now associated with the Left Bank had already set up home there. On the other side of the Boulevard Raspail Edith Wharton, who arrived in Paris in 1906, set herself up in emulation of the old Faubourg salons, partly in order to gain entry to that social world. Wharton, a foreigner like Stein, infiltrated the Parisian *haut monde* and to some extent made it more cosmopolitan. Stein on the other hand, when she first arrived in Paris, was neither wealthy nor well-connected, and the truly well-to-do would not have touched her with a bargepole (that included Edith Wharton – the two women lived a stone's throw away from each other for fourteen years and never met, though they had many friends and acquaintances in common[4]).

The Steins' indifference to protocol, their eccentricity and conspicuous Americanness roused antipathy, and anti-Semitism, in some. Stein of course knew that she was *persona non grata* in certain circles. This was partly because she was American, partly because she was Jewish and partly because she was middle class. That was why, after *The Autobiography*, when she had the pick of Hollywood's own glitziest social strata as dinner companions, she made a point of distinguishing between what she had had before and this new-found fame: finally, she said, she was able to choose who she met.

The Steins' salon was far less formal than Wharton's. In *The Autobiography* Stein refers to her habitués as being of 'all degrees of wealth and poverty'; she also makes a point of adding that 'there was no social privilege attached to knowing anyone there'.[5] It was all done by connections – people brought along their friends, and the question would be put: 'de la part de qui venez-vous?'[6] One simply had to give a name to gain admittance, though even this was a mere formality. When in the 1920s Stein's reputation was fixed and her home had become a place of pilgrimage, the occasional aristocrat would happen by. The Infanta Eulalia of Spain found the people 'delightful' but the pictures 'horrors!'[7] (Stein: 'Somebody brought the Infanta Eulalia and brought her many times.'[8]) In 1908 Mary Cassatt, the American painter, had turned away in disgust, with the words:

> I have never in my life seen so many dreadful paintings in one place; I have never seen so many dreadful people gathered together and I want to be taken home at once.[9]

She was clearly expecting something more decorous from a Paris salon. Stein, happily subversive, was amused by such reactions. Many were appalled at the paintings on the Steins' walls, and some came on purpose to ridicule or deride them.

In its first bloom the Steins' salon was a product of the belle époque, and in reality, despite their eccentricity, they were far from being a couple of brash parvenus. Stein objected to the millionaire American collector Albert Barnes, for example, on the grounds that he came to the atelier and 'did literally wave his cheque book in the air'.[10] In the first years of the Steins' Saturday evenings, theirs was an artistic salon, the focus of the edification was to see the strange and shocking paintings, and to listen to Leo's explanation of them. In *Everybody's Autobiography* Stein writes that in those early years she was silent in the face of Leo's dominance. The literature Gertrude Stein was producing was a back-room business. But by 1910 Stein was in charge. The salon took on a more literary atmosphere, as Gertrude Stein's salon, *sans* Leo. She would take and mould the salon they had started together and fashion it into the myth of her own making.

Stein's was a most 'twentieth-century' salon. For visitors it 'became a kind of American oasis on the banks of the Seine'.[11] It was a mass-market version of the salon at which pretty much everyone was welcome if they had an interest – visitors were trooping through in their hundreds even by 1913 and before the influx of Americans that the war brought. It was in fact more hectic before Alice stepped in and brought an element of decorum. It was an American salon in Paris, and Stein was a great declaimer on the subject of American democracy, but to say that Stein democratized the Parisian salon is going too far, because her gatherings were also all about choosing an elite; the writer Solita Solano, who was not asked to return, said sourly that they were 'well-sieved'.[12] But her elite was of a more idiosyncratic sort, not based on wealth or social standing. While salons had always fostered a certain egalitarian mingling – to a limited extent, the privacy of the salon made it a place where the classes could mix – she seemed an anomalous person to be taking charge of salon culture, being Jewish, American, middle class, with a doctor's education.

In fact Stein belongs to an illustrious line of Jewish salonières in Europe, stretching back to the eighteenth century; there was, too, the salon of the Jewish Ada Leverson in 1890s London; after the First World War, the Jewish artist Florine Stettheimer (who in the 1930s designed the striking sets for Stein's opera *Four Saints in Three Acts*) held a salon in New York, modelled on the Steins'.[13] 'Brother Singulars we are misplaced in a generation that knows not

Joseph . . . we fly to the kindly comfort of an older world', Stein wrote in 1903, self-conscious about the project of creating a new American bohemia in Europe. In Stein's case, the fact that she was from somewhere else meant that she attracted other people from other places; her own anomaly brought anomalies to her door. Being a woman, a Jew and a lesbian was synonymous in the discourse of the day with inferiority, subversiveness and degeneracy. Being an American, for Stein, was an identity that could be used to blot out and supersede all other classifications. She may have been providing a Parisian refuge for unconventional America, but she also used her distance from the country to make a novelty of her own Americanness, and to attest that precisely that unconvention was an American quality. She never relinquished her claim to an American literary tradition.

If being an expatriate American had allowed her to supplant class and ethnic classifications, just as it did for other expats in Paris, this also encompassed strange new gender identities. Stein cites Picasso's comment on the people he encountered at the Steins': 'They are not men, they are not women they are Americans.'[14] 27 rue de Fleurus became a home for those who considered themselves strangers and foreigners, refugees from conformity. Stein used her own marginality to the most extravagant effect. She was the epitome of unconventionality. She took advantage of the power of her exclusion, becoming the motherly mentor of all who could not find a home elsewhere. She attracted those of unexalted backgrounds, a cosmopolitan bunch of alienated souls. She was a natural show-off, and her famous laugh, her *joie de vivre* and the warmth of her reception when she liked you were enough to make you want to come back, and bring your friends.

In the expat milieu, as of old, the salon was an introduction to Paris society, but now it was a new society, a multinational artistic community.[15] Partly because of social phenomena like the salon, visual artists and writers had more opportunity and inclination for

The 'Picasso chairs', embroidered by Alice.

interaction in those days. It was a forum for little magazines, small presses and new collaborations, exchanges of ideas between those at work in different media. What went on at the Steins' was philosophical debate, art appreciation and intellectual conversation. It wasn't just tittle-tattle, as Stein's later populist memoirs might suggest. She also gave advice which according to Natalie Clifford Barney was always immediate and pertinent. Barney called her 'the most affirmative person I have ever met' – and she must have met a few, being the hostess of the main rival salon in Paris.[16] Stein gave people real answers to real problems when they came to her with them. (At her suggestion, Ernest Hemingway went to Spain, Paul Bowles went to Tangier and Richard Wright came to live in Paris.) It was also of course a meeting place, both an enjoyable gathering and a way of being seen and heard. It was held not in a grandly proportioned drawing room, but rather a medium-sized, cosy living space, where you were given liqueur and homemade cakes.

Hemingway said: 'It was like one of the best rooms in the finest museum except there was a big fireplace and it was warm and comfortable.'[17] Her 'at homes' were just that, held from the home, and a sign of her outward-looking character that sits strangely with her internalized writings. They brought 'genius' into a domestic setting, just as the chairs on which they sat were lovingly embroidered by Alice Toklas from designs by Picasso. The salon was both a public and a private place, encouraging both commonality and intimacy. Some impecunious writers went because, apparently, 'the teas were bountiful',[18] and others went to gawp at the spectacle. There were no formal readings, though guests might be treated to an extract from Stein's work. Stein's dominance was above all reliant on the traditional salonière's metier: conversation and the rule of wit.

In the early days there was the core of regulars, with a changing group of guests, as in a traditional salon. Stein has given us some of the most vivid tableaux of the era; in the legend, she created comedic gems such as 1908's 'Rousseau banquet', a real event which was recorded in the memoirs of various participants; in her version this dinner held to celebrate the Douanier Rousseau (Henri Rousseau the painter) became a comic burlesque of the times, an absurd and joyful excrescence of the moment, at which poets and painters joined in a drunken revel, and somebody ate Alice's hat – the main suspect being the poet André Salmon, although in real life it was probably a donkey called Lolo from the Lapin Agile. When she made a party into a symbol of an entire epoch, one of the legends she was helping to create was that this was a time and a place not just of bacchanalian abandon, but of self-conscious myth-making. The idea that her telling of these 'charming stories' relied on was that here self-invention was not only possible but necessary; one remade one's own life story, one told it over and over again until it seemed truer than the real one. She gave herself that licence, and made it part of her myth of bohemia. The French concept of *redoublement* would be precious to Stein, whose work often repeats itself in leitmotifs, refrains, and repetitive scenarios.

A bastion of oral culture before the dawn of the television age, the salon was a place for talking, for friendship, and giving and receiving confidences, all seen as feminine skills. Stein was a great listener as well as a talker. Later her salon became a place where younger writers were brought to pay homage to Stein, purely because of the legend that had sprung up around her, hoping for intimate individual chats. Many commented on the beauty of Stein's voice, which is preserved in recordings she made of such works as 'A Valentine to Sherwood Anderson' (the very title of which draws attention to Stein's use of charm and favour in her work and in the marketing of her work).

Stein's work is far more oral than other modernisms, and perhaps that is related to her skill in the 'feminine' art of conversation. She invested the spoken word with authority. Conversation has, indeed, been seen as 'one of Stein's great forms'.[19] When she addresses the reader it is also as a listener, 'my receiver' – like a telephone receiver. Her work is often more intelligible when off the page: when it was converted into operas and ballets, when she herself delivered lectures, when it is read aloud (take the annual marathon New Year readings of *The Making of Americans* that took place in New York until recently, for example). Her plays, she insisted, must be performed before they were published. Her work also recognizes the value of ephemeral talk.[20] It benefits from being read, its rhythms are those of speech. Stein revived the nineteenth-century idea of conversation as an art-form. Sometimes she would read aloud from her own work to her devotees, or get them to read it to her, as Paul Bowles remembered; she would listen appreciatively to the sentences she herself had constructed, and applaud the bits that struck her as particularly good. The salon was after all Stein's audience – and for a long time she had more of an audience than she did a readership – and also replaced a family home.

Her sociability had an artistic function. *The Making of Americans* came directly from the character studies that derived from her hours of listening, and from that came the portraits and the rest of her mature output. There were several different languages in use at the salon, and it was all grist to Stein's mill. Conversation propelled her prose, and the salon gave her countless subjects for her portraits and novels. The literary portrait itself was traditionally a genteel art form practised by the salonière, while *The Autobiography of Alice B. Toklas* is both about the salon and influenced by the voice of the salon. It reproduces the salon world in its idiom as much as its subject matter.

After the First World War Paris filled with Americans fleeing prohibition and taking advantage of the exchange rate, and Gertrude Stein was surrounded by her countrymen again for the first time since she had left America. The new generation flocked to visit the now-renowned Miss Stein – she had always promoted the arts, not just art, but now there was a new incarnation of Stein's salon that became more literary and more American. By the 1920s the salon was no longer based around the Saturdays; Stein would be in every afternoon from five o'clock onwards, and people dropped in as they pleased. Throughout the 1920s and '30s young men made their pilgrimages to the shrine of Gertrude Stein and she coined the term 'lost generation' in description of them, while for them she was the embodiment of Left Bank bohemia come to life. She had become a mythical personage.

After the war social nicety, punctilio and protocol no longer had the same meanings, and traditional salon culture disappeared. Stein, in any case, had never been one for *politesse* (although she still had her rules). While a stereotypical hostess would be keen to engage and please her guests, Stein did not pander to anyone else's idea of how she should behave. The painter Maurice Grosser wrote: 'She was not at all the gracious and ingratiating hostess she is usually pictured to be. To the contrary, she was brusque, self-assured, and jolly.'[21] (Alice, on the other hand, was most certainly a born host-ess.) She spoke her down-to-earth American English; she dressed bizarrely; if she didn't like you, you knew it immediately. One read-ing of the partnership sees Alice as the salonière, who orchestrated everything for Stein as her main literary lion, taking on the role of a Marcel Proust or an Anatole France. Stein had no patronage to offer, except the cachet of being with her. She created her own mystique and became her own salon's greatest draw. Gertrude Stein helped turn the cultural work of the nineteenth-century salon, which had always been a private institution, into part of the twentieth-century publicity machine. Self-interest guided her own flair for self-publicizing, but in promoting herself through her salon she also contributed to a new era of image management and marketing of personalities. The new mass media made the old networks the salons encouraged into a forum for a new kind of celebrity.[22]

Stein was a canny manipulator of her own public image, at a time when these things were not ruled over by publishing companies and marketing strategists. She paid close attention to the way her work was printed and packaged, insisting on fine paper and bindings, so that the finished product was a beautiful object. She fetishized her own self-published work, according to Toklas's expensive tastes. She used her famous contacts when for example Man Ray's photography graced *The Autobiography of Alice B. Toklas*, or Cecil Beaton provided the dust-jacket image for *Wars I Have Seen*. Just as an earlier salon hostess would often have a portrait of herself as the '*belle savante*', done by one of the frequenters of the salon,[23] Stein was seen to best effect in front of Picasso's portrait of her. Early on Stein had bought Marie Lauren-cin's portrait of the habitués of the salon – Apollinaire, Picasso, Fernande Olivier and Laurencin herself. She made no disguise of her attachment to the outward accoutrements of fame, and before mass media her paintings were the most appropriate signs of her status. They, like the salon itself, were her marketing tools.

Marie Laurencin, *Group of Artists*, 1908, oil on canvas.

There were sculptures by Lipchitz (1920) and Davidson (1922). There were busts by various young American sculptors, and photographs by Man Ray, later a portrait by Picabia. Recent critics have objected to the way in which Stein's physical characteristics – her weight, her supposed androgyny – infiltrated the early discussions of her work.[24] But Stein herself encouraged the dissemination of her own image as part of her literary persona. When she wrote *Everybody's Autobiography*, she used as the frontispiece a photograph with the caption: 'Gertrude Stein, wearing the dress in which she delivered her lectures in America.'[25] She also changed the face of female 'genius', by moving away from norms of femininity both in her person and in her work. Wyndham Lewis's memorable description of Stein as 'a monument sitting on patience'[26] owes its aptness to the fact that through her physical presence she had become an idol, an icon.

She was, in the time-honoured role of the salonière, a creator of other people's literary reputations. She was part of the tourist trail, particularly for any young man wanting to make it as a writer. In November 1919 the American Sylvia Beach opened her bookshop Shakespeare and Company in the nearby rue de l'Odéon. Stein was the first to subscribe to its lending library (although according to Beach this was just a goodwill gesture, and she didn't take an interest in the books). Sylvia Beach would act as an introducer of Stein's fans to her (there was still enough sense of protocol to require that somebody did the introducing): 'the poor things would come to me, exactly as if I were a guide from one of the tourist agencies, and beg me to take them to see Gertrude Stein.'[27] Stein was as well-visited as a monument or a museum.

It was a performance, and was not entirely healthy for Stein as a writer. Although the central pillar of her reputation was her

Sitting for
Jo Davidson,
photographed by
Man Ray, 1922.

Francis Picabia, *Gertrude Stein*, 1933.

innovation ('the "innovator" legend' she had thrust upon her, Robert McAlmon carped) she was now seen as the older generation. Sherwood Anderson was one of the young men who now claimed her as an influence. He had discovered her in 1914 before writing his *Winesburg, Ohio*, which was a bestseller in 1919, and in Paris in 1921 he was determined to meet the writer who he already saw as a mentor. She would continue to act as his instructor, and the following year he wrote a rapturous introduction to her *Geography and Plays*. He became one of her most loyal friends and facilitators. He had imagined her reclining on a chaise longue, sipping absinthe and surveying the world through jaded eyes; the woman he met could not have been more different from the image that had been contrived of her in America.

The young men Sylvia Beach brought along were invariably scared of Stein's formidable reputation. In March 1922 the same was true of Ernest Hemingway, who had arrived in Paris the previous December. He was to become the new doyen of her court. Young Hemingway's demure, grateful letters to her are a surprise. She wrote about their master/student relationship in 'Objects Lie on a Table'. He was never reticent about stating how she had helped create the Hemingway style, partly through her advice – both literary and personal, partly as he emulated her written work (for example in 'Mr and Mrs Elliot', quite a close relative of Stein's 'Miss Furr and Miss Skeene') and partly because she opened his eyes to various aspects of bohemian living (most obviously played out in his story 'The Sea Change', about a young man's sudden, jealous contact with lesbianism). In 1923 she wrote a portrait of Hemingway called 'He and They, Hemingway'. She encouraged him and gave him practical advice, as well as lecturing him on principles of composition, on rhythm and repetition. In 1923 she and Alice became godmothers to Hemingway's first baby. According to Stein, Hemingway listened to and looked at her, and handed over all his work for her appraisal. 'I have a weakness for Hemingway', she said.[28]

Other American visitors in the 1920s included Hart Crane and Thornton Wilder; the latter became one of Stein's closest friends who, in 1974, remembered that 'she was *the* great influence on my life.'[29] By the early twenties Cubism was 'dead'; and Dada had been born (in its literary incarnation nothing much to do with Stein, although newspapers facetiously labelled her 'the mama of Dada' because of her association with visual artists like Picabia and Duchamp) and Surrealism was the latest thing (Stein thought it essentially old-fashioned, unchallenging). She took up with Jean Cocteau and Erik Satie, Picasso's new friends. Stein said that Cocteau had been the 'first French writer to speak of her work'; he liked her work and claimed that it influenced him, though in effect their relationship went very little further than mutual flattery.[30] Each saw the usefulness of being associated with the other.

The rue de Fleurus became a meeting place of egos partly by serendipity and partly because Stein was a networker extra-ordinaire. Her fairly mercenary attitude to acquaintances, her indisputable careerism and her egotism were all defining factors. And she was, after all, blindly ambitious, although she presented a magnanimous, serene face to the world. Equally, the people who came were sometimes more interested in themselves and what kudos she could offer them than in her or her writing. It was known that she could make literary reputations. She wielded her power judiciously, and was careful not to invite people who might undermine, embarrass, or doubt her, or anyone who might usurp her – like Pound or Joyce. (When Pound asked to come and see her again, having recently broken one of her chairs, she claimed to have dismissed him with the words: 'I am so sorry . . . but Miss Toklas has a bad tooth and besides we are busy picking wild flow-ers.'[31]) She gradually filtered out anyone who wasn't an absolute believer in her. T. S. Eliot objected to her on the grounds that she only expected 'devotion and faith'. Any other attitude was, he thought, intolerable to her.[32] The salon was an important social network that involved a great deal of mutual stoking of one another's egos: which also led to back-stabbing. Stein by this time was also stocking up well on ex-friends. 'How did you quarrel with so many all at once?!!!' Carl Van Vechten asked her incredulously.[33]

She inspired rivalries among her followers, such as that between Van Vechten and Wilder. Hemingway said she never spoke well of any other writers unless they could advance her cause in some way. The only exceptions, he claimed, were Scott Fitzgerald and Ronald Firbank.[34] There is no record of any meeting with Firbank. Fitzgerald held her in the high, affectionate and slightly daunted regard of an apostle; he sent her a copy of *Tender Is the Night* when it was published, with the inscription: 'Is this the book you asked for?'[35]

This was her dream: to find herself among male artists and intellectuals – and conquer them. It was a reversal of the salon hostess's traditional role, to enhance the men's conversation and advertise their achievements. Stein's work was on a separate tack from male modernism, and above it, in her own mind. She set herself up as a 'teacher', a charming pedagogue, more a mentor than a traditional society hostess. Her favourites, in the courtly sense, were mainly men. She loved being loved. She enjoyed most people's images, interpretations, and constructions of her, even when they were slightly derogatory (like Skinner, Sitwell, Zangwill) – because she was so interested in herself, she revelled in other people's interest in her. But to be fair to Stein, she also had an enormous, insatiable interest in other people.

She threw parties at which people kowtowed to her primadonna-ish behaviour. She was famous for teasing her male guests, her delight in making others squirm. She would ask people if they had read *The Making of Americans* (not the most commonly achieved of feats even in her circle), and when they said yes, she would ask them their opinion of a particular passage on a particular page, knowing full well that they would be unable to answer. Her baiting of the young men around her was like an intellectual parlour game. Sylvia Beach claimed that 'Gertrude Stein had so much charm that she could often, though not always, get away with the most monstrous absurdities.'[36] Paul Bowles remembered being chased round the garden of Stein's country house in Bilignin by Basket the famous poodle (the ostensible reason was to dry out the wet poodle after his bath), dressed in a pair of lederhosen, known as his 'Faunties', that Stein had made him wear, as she shouted at him 'Faster, Freddy, faster!' (she insisted on calling him Freddy), and when he asked if he could stop: 'No! Keep going!' Bowles: 'There was no way of doubting that she enjoyed my discomfort. But . . . I was flattered by the degree of her interest.'[37] They all endured it. Partly because of the 'cajoling ways' she had learnt in childhood – a charm she ascribed to being the youngest child, that never left her[38] – and partly because to hang out with Gertrude and Alice was to have arrived on the Paris scene.

Stein and Toklas's techniques included snobbery and favouritism – for example Alice Toklas called the Russian painter Pavel Tchelitchew 'a dreadful little arriviste' (after he had done portraits of both of them and the dog).[39] Alice's hostility to some could be intimidating. Picasso's mistress Françoise Gilot said her voice was like 'the sharpening of a scythe'.[40] She was also the preserver of the salon's good manners. Hemingway satirized this as being struck over the head with a bicycle pump by the maid in order to get him to leave. 'Miss Stein was always charming', he adds, and in this context the word 'charming' becomes as catty a veiled insult as she ever dealt him.[41] 'Charming' is even more obviously a pejorative term in his spoof 'Autobiography of Alice B. Hemingway',[42] 'charm' being a feminine skill equated with dissimulation. Hemingway said that Stein 'had such a personality that when she wished to win anyone over to her side she could not be resisted.'[43] She could deliver stinging judgements to people's faces and they wouldn't mind, if she was smiling – as Bowles recalled. That was

Stein and Picasso in Stein's garden at Bilignin, *c.* 1930.

partly because her relationships were self-serving on both sides. In this way she kept up the role of motherly, teasing, flirtatious mistress of ceremonies, as well as the main attraction. Those she kept around her were eager to please. The main criterion for being asked back was an ability to scintillate, not necessarily any talent.

There was a certain flippancy and fleetingness to the culture which she encouraged. 'Give me new faces new faces new faces I have seen the old ones', she wrote, quoting a favourite song of Alice's, in *Everybody's Autobiography*.[44] Stein and her salon could be seen as a step along literature's way to becoming a commodity, a tributary of show business.[45] Carl Van Vechten, one of her most loyal subjects, who she named as her literary executor in her will, wrote without embarrassment after her death about their relationship: 'We talked little of her work, although we often read it.'[46] (This probably says more about Van Vechten, a promoter, publicist and party animal, than it does about Stein.) Such frivolity, typical as it was of salon discourse, was also implicitly a feminine attribute. Being a 'liar' as Leo, the 'Testimony Against Gertrude Stein' which appeared in *Transition*, and, in a sidelong way, Hemingway, accused her of being, was almost part of the trade. There was a slippery and somewhat untrustworthy quality that belonged to charm. Stein's word experiments were another facet of this. Her playfulness and her relativism – the fact that her work is not about truth, just about process – also make them untrustworthy. But shallowness and surface were not the values she deliberately fostered. When she wrote *The Autobiography* she could hardly forgive herself for the gossip it seemed to glorify. Nevertheless the book, the salon and the image of Stein herself fed into the growing consumer culture surrounding the arts in general. As she magisterially pronounced in *The Autobiography of Alice B. Toklas*, 'everybody came and no one made any difference.'[47]

By now there were other rival expatriate salons, and the old private cliques that prospered in the drawing rooms of the Faubourg mansions were no longer relevant to a dynamic, democratic café society that relished publicity and wanted as big an audience as possible. In the expat community everyone knew what everyone else was doing. Stein did not frequent the café scene, which was where much of Parisian society had moved; she let it come to her. There were other contemporary women who filled the role of salonière at one time or other – Bloomsbury hostesses including Lady Ottoline Morell, ambitious writers and social butterflies such as Violet Hunt, society ladies like Nancy Cunard. These three themselves each paid visits to Stein's atelier. Following Stein's lead, Mabel Dodge initiated her fairly short-lived Wednesday evenings in Greenwich Village in 1913. In the 1920s Sylvia Beach's bookshop also functioned as a salon of sorts.

The other main Parisian salon was Natalie Clifford Barney's. Barney arrived in Paris in 1902, a year before Stein. Her regular meetings were held on Fridays. Barney's salon was a meeting place for lesbians, but she also held another version at which everyone was welcome. Sapphic parties were held in the back garden, and a literary salon in the drawing room, and she held formal evenings at which writers were inducted into her 'academy of women'.

Stein's finances were not in the same league as those of the heiresses Barney and Cunard. One of the things she counselled Hemingway about was financial prudence, although she didn't need a job, so there was financial freedom of a sort – more than Hemingway had. Stein's salon was a middle-class salon. Neither was hers a lesbian salon, a community of women writers in the manner of Barney and Renée Vivien, or Sylvia Beach and Adrienne Monnier. In *The Autobiography* Stein mentions Barney, as well as her friend the Duchess of Clairmont Tonnerre, one of the sights of 'Paris-Lesbos'.[48] But Stein's was, in fact, a remarkably heterosexual salon.

Barney promoted other Left Bank writers, and women writers in particular, giving them opportunities to circulate their work. Stein, in contrast, preferred male writers, and her salon was more concerned with self-promotion.[49] Gertrude Stein was not a promoter of others, but of herself, and she didn't see the salon as a forum for women's rights, just her own. (There is also the fact that biographers have preferred to dwell on her relationships with male contemporaries rather than her relationships with women.) Barney's was probably more magnanimous and less self-serving. Though the two were friends who enjoyed a walk in the park together, Stein did not as a rule venture to Barney's evenings, though she made an exception in order to attend an evening celebrating herself in 1927, featuring Mina Loy and Ford Madox Ford, and 200-odd assorted admirers.

Stein was not a fan of chivalry – mainly because she wanted to be treated as a man – or etiquette – she made up her own rules. One of these was the seemingly bizarre habit of having Alice usher the wives out of earshot so she could convene with the great men alone. Alice would preside over the tea table and talk about hats and perfume with the women. This vetting process was one traditional piece of salon culture that Stein preserved, and was quite the opposite of Barney's lesbian get-togethers. Djuna Barnes's hostile reaction to Stein was partly due to this chauvinism, as she saw it.

Sylvia Beach thought the 'cruelty to wives'[50] was odd on the grounds that it only applied to wives, rather than girlfriends, mistresses or other female companions. Perhaps the reason was simply that most of writers who came were male, and Stein was naturally interested in speaking to them rather than anyone else they had brought along. Banishing the wives allowed her to promote herself more persuasively among influential men, without the possibility of contradiction from a rival female. They joked that Alice's autobiography should be called 'Wives of Geniuses I Have Sat With'. Stein categorically wanted to guard her own place among the geniuses. Bravig Imbs, the writer and devotee of the Stein salon, explained that Alice acted as a 'sieve and buckler. She defended Gertrude from the bores and most of the new people were strained through her before Gertrude had any prolonged conversation with them.'[51] Alice also (according to Maurice Grosser), if she got very bored of the wife or girlfriend, would 'enlist Gertrude's help to try to make the pair break up'.[52]

Stein's salon was of course flourishing at a time when new liberties were flourishing for women. It was a feminine calling, but it was also the perfect role for her, she who had seen herself as an anomaly, a masculine woman, one who preferred the company of men to women. She could be of them and above them. The traditional salon had always been an area where women could have an influence, albeit surreptitious. Everything rotated around the salonière. Without a voice in print, she could dish out criticism at will. Stein too was very patchily published, and her print voice was nothing like as well known as it is now, thanks to the posthumous publication of her uncollected writing. But her role as a hostess allowed her to become a senior figure in the Paris literary scene, dispensing her judgements on a world that was still failing to take her work seriously. It made her, eventually, part of the establishment.

The attendance of Anderson and Hemingway meant the years between 1918 and 1925 were something of a boom; suddenly her work was being published. The new atmosphere in Paris gave her new opportunities as well as new competition for her status as the chronicler of 'the relationship of consciousness to language'.[53] Obviously trying to keep up to date, in 1920 she wrote something called 'A Movie'; in 1929 she also wrote a film scenario called 'Film Deux Soeurs Qui Ne Sont Pas Soeurs' – the first thing written in French she had ever published. In a piece called 'I feel a really anxious moment coming' she wrote about X-rays.[54] New technologies had entered her line of consciousness. In the mid-1920s she turned to America again as subject matter, and became preoccupied again with the idea of a novel, which she had veered from in the previous decade. Examples of her later novels range from *Lucy Church Amiably* (a 'pastoral' novel) to 'a short novel'. What is more, she began for the first time to explain herself, which she had never done before in her writing. Later in her lectures she would become practically a full-time explainer of her own work.

In 1922 *Geography and Plays* (a luminous compilation of some of her unpublished experimental works) was published with Anderson's introduction. Hemingway persuaded an unsuspecting Ford Madox Ford to begin serial publication of *The Making of Americans* in *The Transatlantic Review*. Now her short pieces were appearing with some regularity in *The Little Review*, *Vanity Fair* and *Transition*. It was also Hemingway who secured the long hoped-for publication of *The Making of Americans*; his friend Robert McAlmon finally published it in his imprint Contact Editions in 1925. The spectacle of Anita Loos and Gertrude Stein signing *Gentleman Prefer Blondes* and *The Making of Americans* together in a Paris bookshop must have been something to behold.

When McAlmon fell out with Stein over getting her book into print, he wrote an anonymous parody – which he cuttingly called a 'portrait' – of Stein. Here he reported her as saying: 'the Jews have produced only three originative geniuses: Christ, Spinoza, and myself.'[55] Behind her back, many people were fed up with the atmosphere of hero-worship surrounding Stein. Pound later published the parody in *Exile* in 1938 and the words went down as if they were really hers. Many were beginning to see her as a false idol – and a very demanding one. It was perhaps a natural reaction to mistrust someone so ostentatiously charming.

However celebrated it made her, and however great the company, seeing herself as a salonière, a nurturer of male authors and artists, detracted from her serious reputation. But this also made her a creator of culture. This was a double bind of her own making. She publicized herself, and for that she was admonished by contemporaries. Many had a false impression of her as a mere socialite. Michael Gold, the mouthpiece of proletarian literature, weighed into her in a piece called 'Gertrude Stein: A Literary Idiot' in *The New Masses*. His was a false image of her as an idle, wealthy dilettante, whose writing resembled 'the monotonous gibberings of paranoiacs in the private wards of asylums'.[56] Stein, seen as the fat, moneyed decadent, the irresponsible bourgeois artist lazily perverting the common language, wasn't popular with the radical political writers of the 1930s. Ironically, a more right-wing critical reaction would also see her as a symbol of cultural degeneration. In the 1950s B. L. Reid epitomized that tradition when he spat out his now well-known final judgement: 'Later ages will gather about the corpus of her work like a cluster of horrified medical students around a biological sport.'[57]

Many contemporary discussions and parodies of her work mix up judgements about Stein's body with imputations of mental illness or insanity, and babyishness, all adding up to the sort of degeneracy that she was seen to represent, the degenerate and hedonistic life of Americans in Paris. She got people's backs up; many readers actually found her writing offensive, although – and because – as they invariably stated, they couldn't understand it. Lampooning reviews appeared with titles such as 'Officer, she's writing again' (a review of *Tender Buttons*); 'Incitement to Riot' (a 1923 review of *Geography and Plays*); and 'Miss Stein Applies Cubism to Defenceless Prose' (also 1923, in which the writer suggests that Stein is 'ready for occupational therapy').[58] Her writing genuinely upset people. They called her insane, indolent, infantile, fat, Jewish, female. And they directly transposed these judgements to her writing.[59] Even Edmund Wilson, at one point an admirer, referred to the 'fatty degeneration of her imagination and style' and to some of her prose as 'echolaliac incantations . . . half-witted-sounding catalogues'.[60]

Stein was no hedonist. She lived a temperate life, though she enjoyed good food and accepted good things when they came to her. She had wild dreams of making money from her work, but by the 1920s she didn't really expect to. Her art was the thing which made her herself, it was the axis of her life. In fact, very far from one image of her as a fat, pampered baby or indolent socialite, one of the most striking things about her writing life is its extraordinary energy. (An energy that makes it nigh on impossible to briefly sum up her style, because she had so many of them.) She was no sphinx without a secret, she was an extraordinarily gifted communicator, which is what, for a contemporary public, made it so very alarming and intriguing that she chose to write in a way that often could not be understood. She had an artistic mission to fulfil that went beyond being an instructor or a facilitator for others – she wanted to lead the way. Her reservations about the cynical exercise of writing a bestseller in the 1930s were heartfelt soul-searching, and as such are touching. Her joyful appreciation of the money she earned was tempered with reservations about putting herself on the market and a distrust of writing for what she called 'the buyer'.

The salon was certainly the forum for her to hone her biting wit, but separating the louche diction of the salonière – the epigrammatic backbone of the autobiography's humour – from the self-questioning of the experimental writer is important. Her work (the novels, portraits, plays and poetry she was writing throughout the 1920s) was moving on apace, ever more outlandish and idio-syncratic, hermetic, while her life became more and more sociable. It was no act of wilfulness for one so patently able to express her-self with formidable clarity to choose such obscure routes to making herself understood. She felt compelled to do so. It was only possible to explain her work by using the method of expression in which it was written. (That said, calling a piece as difficult as it is 'An Elucidation' is clearly perverse.)

Those who saw her as an infantile writer, or a degenerate one, unwittingly laid bare the ultimate discrepancy in Stein's public image, between the naive writer and the effete 'genius'. The tough-ness of much of Stein's work is sometimes hard to triangulate with the almost giddy persona she sometimes gave the world. That she was naturally funny, outgoing and eccentric did not prevent her from turning aside to create works of intimidating austerity. In later works she used her natural humour to good effect and played up that amenable voice. Seldom did she combine the two. But the one impinged on the other in terms of her reception. That other voice plagued her. Stein was the victim of harsh and hostile criticism for many years, while celebrated and cosseted by those who loved her. But the lifestyle, the milieu and the fact that she was a well-known face made it impossible to separate the two Steins. This was confus-ing; her humour was distracting, and detracted from the seriousness with which her literary experiments were received.

Although Stein's work was becoming more widely circulated, critics and reviewers were not debating her writing, but rather whether or not she was serious. In 1924–5 Edith Sitwell became part of the Gertrude Stein fan club. She came to Paris to interview Stein for *Vogue*, and while she was there she tried to persuade Stein to em-bark on a publicity campaign. Stein at first balked at the unsubtlety of the idea, but finally it was agreed that she would travel to England. She called the lecture 'Composition as Explanation' and delivered it in Cambridge and then in Oxford, in 1926. Harold Acton wrote an entertaining account of its reception, contrasting what the young men of Oxford expected of Stein – an exotic decadent – and the shock of the reality of the figure that greeted them. (Stein had in fact gone all out, as usual, to cut a dashing first impression, delivering the lecture in another of her costumes, a robe of blue brocade designed for her by a Parisian couturière.[61]) The lecture audience was also struck by the difference between what she said and the way she said it: her easy, engaging manner, and her difficult prose; the voice that made you feel at home, and the words that made you feel at sea. 'Nobody had heard anything like this before', Acton wrote. Some members of the audience were offended by her words, and verbally attacked her in the two hours of questions and answers that followed. She dealt with them beautifully, attended by 'her tall bodyguard of Sitwells and the gypsy acolyte' (Alice).[62] She was a hit. She felt 'just like a prima donna'.[63] Her own amusement and bafflement at her new-found status was telling. Her reputation was not coldly engineered; it was against her nature to be so gauche as to go all out for publicity, and yet she did have a way of winning people over that was one of her greatest talents.

At this stage of her career Stein was better known for the parodies of her work that appeared in *Life* and *Vanity Fair* than for her work itself. She was a sitting duck. Lord Berners, who became a friend, did clever pastiches of Stein for the London papers. (He also later wrote the score for Stein's ballet, *A Wedding Bouquet*, which was produced at Sadlers Wells with Margot Fonteyn and Ninette de Valois.) At least, she ruefully retorted, 'my sentences do get under their skin'.[64]

Back in Paris, James Joyce's *Ulysses* was now taking centre stage. Although she and Joyce were the two great literary personalities in Paris at the time, they didn't meet until 1930, when Sylvia Beach introduced them. They shook hands, exchanged stilted pleasantries, and went their separate ways. Stein was jealous of Joyce, and disapproved of *Ulysses* for her usually idiosyncratic reasons, but partly because she saw it as usurping the glory of *The Making of Americans*. Stein's *A Book Concluding with As a Wife Has a Cow: A Love Story* was published in 1926, another vanity arrangement, illustrated with Juan Gris' lithographs. Leonard Woolf's Hogarth Press published *Composition as Explanation*. She wrote a 'translation' of Georges Hugnet's 'Enfances' that was in fact a separate work, which cut out all the distastefulness in Hugnet's poem (though it was about sex and death), and which led to one of those unbreachable sorts of rifts in which Stein's friendships so often terminated. The cause of the disagreement, interestingly, was Stein's insistence that she should get 'top billing' on the book's cover. She still craved acceptance. By the example of those she had nurtured, from Picasso to Hemingway, Stein was beginning to grasp the way to disseminate herself to an even wider public.

Seven

It is a great paradox that the woman known as one of the most hermetic writers of the twentieth century also became a media figure and a celebrity author. In 1932, aged 58, she wrote *The Autobiography of Alice B. Toklas*, and late in life Gertrude Stein experienced the most intriguing twist in her career: her book was a bestseller and made her a star. Her stardom came at a time when the nature of fame was changing, through the intervention of Hollywood and newsreels, radio and magazines. In turn it brought the theme of celebrity into her writing. That such an experimental writer should have experienced these changes first hand, so that she was then able to make them the subject of her experimental writing, is one more of the felicitous quirks of fortune in a life filled with them.

Some of Stein's most innovative work in her long writing life was in the realm of autobiography, and even her most experimental poems, fictions and dramas were often autobiographical in genesis. Often, too, they related everyday events and feelings, as if she were using them as an encoded diary. Later she wrote what were officially announced as autobiographical works. Not only *The Autobiography of Alice B. Toklas*, but *Everybody's Autobiography*, *Paris France*, and *Wars I Have Seen* – all were experiments in the art of autobiography and memoir, and played with the generic limits of life writing. Her war memoirs are different again from the rest of her work: another new strand to her Protean style, although she was by then in her seventies.

In a sense all Stein's writing is autobiography – to a far greater extent than can be said for most authors. Because most of her writing is about the nature of identity and how it might adequately be expressed through words, hers is the most self-referential *oeuvre* imaginable: her theme was herself and the workings of her mind. She is her own subject, in the scientific as well as the literary sense. Although in *The Making of Americans* Stein had rejected the possibility of a selective autobiography, most of the material is autobiographical; it is a 'history of me and the kind of suffering I can have in me'.[1] Critics have struggled with a conception that Stein's 'I' must be somehow democratic, like Whitman's, for example.[2]

By the early 1930s she still held to the doctrine that one should write without a readership in mind. Her work was finally gaining a serious critical foothold. *The Dial* had published Marianne Moore's review of *The Making of Americans*, and in 1930 William Carlos Williams wrote a review of 'The Work of Gertrude Stein', published in *Pagany*. The most important step came in 1931 with Edmund Wilson's *Axel's Castle*, a breakthrough because it took her seriously (mentioning her alongside Joyce, Proust and Eliot), and he was a major critic. Sherwood Anderson wrote to her – sycophantically, but with an element of truth: 'anyone who follows writing sees your influence everywhere.'[3] And yet Stein's writing was not going well, she had become unconnected from it, dissatisfied. She was taking stock of her achievements. In 'Forensics' in *How to Write* she claimed, somewhat optimistically: 'At last I am writing a popular novel.' But then added a typically undermining question: 'Popular with whom[?]'[4]

As her renown spread she began to write about fame itself. She wrote numerous plays, one of which was *Four Saints in Three Acts*, a piece commissioned by the composer Virgil Thomson, who would write an opera score for it. (He said that when they met they immediately got on, 'like Harvard men'.[5] The opera was produced in 1934 at the height of her American celebrity.) She had an interest in saints as figures whose legends stood above time, rather like geniuses. She was interested in the idea of how a life became legendary; she herself 'always wanted to be historical'[6] – and she chose as the two main characters Spanish saints Ignatius and Teresa, because they were her 'favourites', rather as if the lives of saints she had been reading were a fun indulgence, like celebrity biographies.[7] She teasingly thought the libretto might get her on the radio and receiving royalties. She was right about her imminent success.

Advised by Jo Davidson, who sculpted the statue of her that now stands in Bryant Park, that she should try to sell her personality, she told him that she thought the public only had a right to be interested in her personality 'in so far as it is expressed in the work'.[8] She was desperately concerned that her work should not be seen as a curiosity. But Stein needed money – in the early 1930s she was forced to sell some of her paintings simply to get money to publish her own work. Gertrude and Alice decided to sell Picasso's *Girl with a Fan* to start their own edition of Stein's work, to be called Plain Edition. (*Lucy Church Amiably* was the first book to be published under this imprint, in 1930.) Stein and Toklas were nothing if not entrepreneurs.

So she decided to write her autobiography, with the deliberate intention of making it a bestseller. She said she wrote *The Autobiography* between October and November 1932, apparently dashing it off in six weeks. (It probably took longer, but she was also writing *Stanzas in Meditation* and other shorter works during the same period.) The publication of this highly readable and entertaining memoir made her famous after a lifetime of being called unreadable. Its deceptively straightforward style floored everyone, fans and critics alike. *The Autobiography of Alice B. Toklas* was a conscious piece of myth- and image-making.

The timing was perfect. *The Autobiography* was the first and most hotly anticipated in a string of revelations of 'legendary women' – to quote Hemingway, who wasn't quite prepared for the stinging treatment he would receive in its pages. Edith Wharton and Mabel Dodge, for example, both published their autobiographies within a year or two of Stein's. In *The Autobiography*, in which Stein got in on the rising tide of celebrity culture, her talents as a raconteuse were made available to all the world; you no longer had to visit her salon to be party to the bitchy, clever, piquant wit.

Stein was a connoisseur of autobiographies and biographies, and had always teased Alice that she should write hers. The device of doing it for her, and using Alice's gossipy voice to do so, was indeed a stroke of genius. Friends had begun to urge Gertrude to write her own autobiography. The reason she kept telling Alice to do it was that she was reluctant to enter into so blatantly commercial an exercise. The apparent *jeu d'esprit* that resulted wrong-foots and good-humouredly disconcerts the reader. When it was first published Stein's name did not appear on the cover; the true identity of the author did not appear until the last, seven-word sentence of the last paragraph:

> About six weeks ago Gertrude Stein said, it does not look to me as if you were ever going to write that autobiography. You know what I am going to do. I am going to write it for you. I am going to write it as simply as Defoe wrote the autobiography of Robinson Crusoe. And she has and this is it.

That the ending was a punchline turned the whole book into an elegant joke. But it was also one of its many punchlines, this 'autobiography' being a comic blend of non-fiction and fiction which artfully uses anecdote, irony, aphorism and paradox to achieve its effects.

It was completely different from anything Stein had ever written before, and this was the book that fixed her legend and her image in the popular imagination. The image of the imperious and daunting Stein is really created, by herself, in the 1930s, with humorous panache. If she had never written *The Autobiography* the glimpses of her that her other writing shows would give a far different impression, and the world would have had a far different idea of Stein. When it became a Book-of-the-Month Club selection in 1933, it was an instant smash hit.

Stein had often used a voice that sounded like Alice's in earlier works, but never to the extent of a full-blown impersonation. Alice B. Toklas's 'autobiography' is written in character. While in other works there was often clash between Stein's narrator and non-narrator selves, the one continually subverting the other, by using Alice's voice in the *Autobiography* she pulled off the one thing she had always avoided writing – a story – with fantastic comic aplomb. It is one of the most successful comic voices of the era. When Alice says for example that, after Stein's Oxford lecture, one young man 'was so moved that he confided to me as we went out that the lecture had been his greatest experience since he had read Kant's *Critique of Pure Reason*',[9] the elaborately guileless voice of Alice B. Toklas becomes part of a humorous tradition that stretches from Huck Finn to Lorelei Lee.[10] The put-downs and pointed asides have the feel of being well-handled, and indeed they were stories that had been honed over the years; they were what Janet Flanner, the *New Yorker*'s resident Parisian, referred to as its 'respoken conversations'.[11] (This also made it quick to write.)

The Autobiography is a commercial book. The story it tells is also a deliberately constructed success story. Stein's cheerful persona probably makes her unique among modernist writers, and like most of Stein's work the autobiography is indefatigably upbeat. Within its pages she stages the moment when her friend H. P. Roché commented that a chance remark of hers would be good for the biography – at which point she records a sudden, romantic, Hollywood-style realization that one day she, Gertrude Stein from Allegheny Pennsylvania, would have a biography. And it becomes a self-fulfilling prophecy, for here it is: Stein's fairytale of success, the 'biography' Stein was looking for, though she cannily avoids mentioning that she has penned it herself.[12] This rags-to-riches story is slightly preposterous, but that is part of its appeal; it tapped into a myth of Parisian bohemia that many American readers wanted to believe in and vicariously enjoy, now that the Depression had curtailed the easy flow of tourists to the city.

Using her Parisian contemporaries as walk-on characters, its subject was, as 'Alice' herself put it, 'the vie de Bohème just as one had seen it in the opera'.[13] By calling it bohemia, as by calling herself a genius, Stein gave herself and everyone else in the book an out of the ordinary licence to behave outrageously, but she tamed it all, brought the misrule into check in the end, by making all her characters middle-class success stories.[14] What Stein managed to do through her perfectly finished anecdotes (none of them too risqué or revealing) was to turn individuals into embodiments of culture – into celebrities – and in fact transformed culture itself into celebrity-watching. After her autobiography America wanted more 'lives of legendary women'; she epitomized a trend that was continued by people like Margherita Sarfatti (the Italian salonière and Benito Mussolini's lover), who wrote their stories in deliberate imitation of Stein's mother of all Paris memoirs. Others, like Robert McAlmon and Ernest Hemingway, wrote in retaliation.

Critics have pointed out the selfishness of making Alice the mouthpiece for Stein's unmitigated self-congratulation and then calling it her 'autobiography'. Though on one level it is a supremely solipsistic device, in reality Alice (who had often acted as a double and an answering voice in the writings) was in on the act from the beginning, helping with drafts and making numerous corrections, perhaps suggesting more serendipitous, or more Alice-like, phrasing. By writing what is essentially her own memoir through the point of view of another, someone who, though she could not have been closer to Stein, only met her when she was already the adult 'Gertrude Stein', Stein avoids having to write about her own childhood. She allows 'Alice' to gloss over this period of her life happily.

Toklas was cast as the innocent abroad, which allowed Stein a faux-naif voice that not only recast all the unpleasant details in a happier light, but gave all her bitchiest observations even more impact for their fragile pretence of wide-eyed innocence.

It also allowed her to enact a simultaneous display and concealment of her lesbian life, to parade and disguise their love. Catharine R. Stimpson, one of Stein's pioneering commentators of the 1980s, questioned the 'decorum' of this strategy – the 'tactfulness' of hovering between letting readers know about their relationship and not letting them know – suggesting it is a kind of 'repression'.[15] It is possible to see Stein's attitude to her own sexuality, as she expressed it in her work, as full of half confessions and deliberate obscuring; if it was so, it was as a product of the culture in which it existed. She flouted convention to the utmost, but she wanted recognition, and she wrote *The Autobiography of Alice B. Toklas* for the mainstream. She gave dainty morsels of their domestic life together, as would a celebrity interview, but never gave away so much that could be completely pieced together. She acted as if she was being completely transparent, all the better to cover up her homosexuality. But at the time Stein's lesbianism was both there for all to see and, because not commented on, almost see-through – and accepted. In illustrating the book, the couple chose impressive images of themselves together and of Stein alone, and interspersed them with images by Picasso and others, packaging themselves as the domestic nurturers of genius, both down to earth and brilliant. The glimpse into their home life satisfied a similar need as a magazine spread or a documentary; it was an early celebrity biography, except that it was written by a serious writer.

Stimpson commented on 'the packaging of homosexuality' in *The Autobiography*, how Stein changed her own 'subversion' into 'entertainment'. As Stimpson argues, calling herself a 'genius' as Stein did neutralizes her other abnormalities (namely her lesbianism), makes them non-threatening, because a genius is not expected to fit in with 'normal' life; it exempts her from 'normal' behaviour without making her 'abnormal' in an unpresentable way.[16] Stein does not include any details of her life in Paris that might be considered shocking – with a mercenary eye on the best-seller market, but it wasn't in her to do so anyway. Because it could not state the actual relationship between the two women, the book could not be 'true', even if any life writing could. It is about her life with Alice Toklas, but it could not talk about the way they lived together. So it is instead a version of their life together. Stein is exceptionally self-reflexive and knowing about the limits of the real in the written word.

The book's comic buoyancy, its relentless way of ignoring any-thing negative – related to Stein's 'charm' – is in fact an outcome of Stein's search for approval and acceptance: not self-confidence at all, but its opposite. She clearly did feel stifled at the same time as trumpeting her achievements, because her anxiety flowed out into *Stanzas in Meditation*. Early on in the autobiography Stein pointedly confesses to being 'a little bitter' at the fact of all her unpublished manuscripts. She had always wanted to create something 'everlasting', and now she was beginning to worry that publication and recognition had not come to her, had passed her by, while those she had encouraged were garnering laurels and becoming public figures. Stein hated solitude. She needed to express herself continually, to communicate herself to others. She was forever building a splendid image of herself and the *Auto-biography* is the apogee of that determination. It can be seen as another portrait, or series of portraits – think of the chapter headings such as 'Gertrude Stein in Paris'; they merge with the photo captions. This self-portrait became, once again, more famous than the real Stein. Here she became a character, living inside an eminently readable book.

In *The Autobiography* she carefully disparaged other writers who might threaten her throne, or to dislodge her crown – Marinetti ('very dull'), Pound ('a village explainer, excellent if you were a village, but if you were not, not'[17]), and, most treacherously, Hemingway. Veiling all with a veneer of politeness, Stein allowed 'Alice' a fugue of barbed observations: Hemingway is 'yellow'; 'he looks like a modern and smells of the museums'; he was created by Gertrude Stein and Sherwood Anderson, 'and they were both a little proud and a little ashamed of the work of their minds'.[18] A mutual friend, Hutchins Hapgood, attributed Stein's bad treatment of Hemingway in *The Autobiography* to the latter's anti-Semitic portrayal of Robert Cohn in *The Sun Also Rises*.[19] Another reason was Hemingway's vicious Sherwood Anderson spoof in *The Torrents of Spring*, which Stein must have seen as ungrateful and disloyal. But even Anderson himself was slightly appalled 'when you took such big patches of skin off Hemmy with your delicately held knife'.[20] The cloaked venom Stein had used against Hemingway also worked for others. *The Autobiography* is full of the most intricate and ladylike put-downs.

The variety of Hemingway's retaliations attests to the depth of his hurt; first he sent Stein a copy of *Death in the Afternoon* inscribed: 'A Bitch is a Bitch is a Bitch is a Bitch. From her pal Ernest Hemingway';[21] then he wrote 'The Autobiography of Alice B. Hemingway' (an unpublished parody); years later he hit out at her again in *A Moveable Feast*; and made various sniping attacks, in print, in correspondence and in conversation to their joint friends and acquaintances. Having fallen out, they carried on a certain grim rapport in their mutual insults. Even so, Hemingway's acknowledgement of Stein's advice was lasting, in a letter to Ezra Pound he wrote in 1933.[22] Stein and Hemingway did apparently make up in the late 1930s. But years later when they met he supposedly said: 'I am old and rich. Let's stop fighting'; to which she retorted: 'I am not old. I am not rich. Let's go on fighting.'[23]

In 1935 came another backlash against *The Autobiography*, in the 'Testimony Against Gertrude Stein', a deputation brought by a squadron of her former friends who, rather missing the point, complained that it wasn't true. Eugene Jolas complained of the book's 'hollow tinsel bohemianism and egocentric deformations'.[24] Matisse complained that she had said his wife looked like a horse. The piece was published in *Transition*.

Stein had a passion for and natural way with irony and paradox in all her work. *The Autobiography of Alice B. Toklas* is a deeply ironic text: an almost self-parodying comment on autobiographical form as well as a funny, easily digestible read. For somebody so obsessed with realism and reality, realness and particularly the realness of identity and character, how could a piece of writing purporting to reveal the 'real' her be anything else? Nobody believed more than Stein that a writer's work was more important than her personality. That is the greatest joke of the book.

With formidable lightness of touch, *The Autobiography* riddles away at the problems of autobiographical form. The book ignored, in fact blatantly disavowed, traditional autobiographical constraints such as modesty. It also undermined traditional ways of coping with time and the necessary distance from oneself as subject matter that exists in most autobiographical narrative. Her writing mixes what she's saying, her subject, with interruptions that happen while she's saying it, or trying to say it. She continued this technique in *Everybody's Autobiography*, where she cut to the heart of the matter with the phrase: 'That is really the trouble with an autobiography . . . you do not really believe yourself why should you'.[25] This is what the 'Testimony Against Gertrude Stein' had naively failed to realize. Stein's book was a semi-fictional portrayal, of course, of great comedic strength. It relied on caricature, of everyone, including herself and Alice. It was written as 'Alice's version of events, not Stein's own. Importantly, 'Gertrude Stein' in the book is seen through wifely eyes; this is deliberately and hilariously not the same view that the dominant literary culture had of Stein. When people think of Stein's proclamations of her own genius in this book they often overlook that, written in character, it is Stein's comment on the reliability of any biographical or autobiographical voice. She always rejected conventional rhetoric, and she continued to do so in the autobiographies.

In fact, Stein very rarely employed any material in her writing that was not culled directly from and concerned directly with her everyday life. In *Tender Buttons* she had begun to mainline the everyday details of her life into her work. In *The Making of Americans* she was writing about the act of writing as she performed it. So it was not flippantly that she converted such strategies into the remarks that turn up in *The Autobiography*, remarks that are highly disruptive to the traditional conception of an autobiography as representing a measured truth, even if only a partial one. In *Alice B. Toklas* and *Everybody's Autobiography* she plays with time frames: 'one just broke this morning . . .';[26] 'In the bath this morning . . .'.[27] She draws attention to the fact that she forgets things, and doesn't mind the fact that her separate accounts contain conflicting information, if one is looking for a factual version of events. She brings her own fabrication and raconteurism into scrutiny. Most cunning of all is the *The Autobiography*'s final sentence, which makes it clear that a sly filtering has taken place. In the last lines of the book, 'Alice' denies having written it, but Gertrude Stein is not speaking either – Stein herself never makes an appearance as author. They have both disowned it.[28] By stating 'I am going to write it as simply as Defoe wrote the autobiography of Robinson Crusoe', Stein/Alice was of course drawing attention to the very un-simplicity of the device. *Robinson Crusoe* was not, of course, an autobiography. She had turned Alice into a fiction, and many of the book's first readers thought Alice no more than a literary device.[29] The ending not merely questions the reliability of the narrator but puts her unreliability up in lights, at the same time as it shows the unreliability of distinctions between fact and fiction, the unreliability of all story-telling. She entices, enthrals and engages with the reader, only to playfully subvert their attentiveness in the final sentence, which allows her to shirk the yoke of conventionality once more.

Later Stein would admit that in writing *The Autobiography of Alice B. Toklas* she had 'lost her personality'.[30] Properly speaking Stein became a personality and lost her identity. Its writing and its reception became a traumatic experience. It was written for a readership, and Stein was not used to writing for a readership. It was in fact probably the first thing she had written for a readership other than Alice. She had apparently told Hemingway – in the same breath as her famous 'remarks are not literature' comment – 'If you have an audience it's not art. If anyone hears you it's no longer pure.'[31] She did not write for anyone's pleasure. (This was also her rationalization of her lack of popular success, her valorization of her status as artistic outlaw.) The reception of *The Autobiography*, however cleverly it was written, made her into light entertainment. Maria Jolas in her testimony used the phrase 'Barnumesque publicity'. Stein packaged herself so successfully that she lost control of herself as a commodity.

Furthermore, if by writing in a voice not her own she could create her most successful book, it made her doubt the value of her own voice. She said of her sudden explosion into narrative that it demonstrated that 'most narrative is based not upon your opinions but upon someone else's'.[32] In a way she had given over her voice and her story to Toklas, and she did not enjoy the experience (just as she always insisted on being the only person allowed on a stage she was to speak on). Questions persist about whether she was emulating Toklas's real voice, and how much of a hand Alice had in the manuscript. In the original edition's photographic illustrations, chosen by Stein, the last illustration is a facsimile of Stein's writing, the final ironic piece of evidence. Early in her career Stein had elaborately rejected the usefulness of a piece of writing in one's own hand as evidence of memory or personality; its use here, just when

The cover of *The Autobiography*, originally published in 1933 by Harcourt Brace.
Photographed by Man Ray.

she was shifting between her own identity and Alice's, is deliberately multivalent and suggestive. (Gertrude and Alice's love story had also started, and been carried out and propelled on paper, via the handwritten words passing between them, as Stein left correspondence, questions and love notes for Alice along with each day's work to be typed up, and Alice responded in writing.) The frontispiece of the book is a photograph by Man Ray of 'Alice B. Toklas at the Door'. It is a photograph of the room, the salon, where the book is being written, as if it has captured Stein while writing the book, although it was actually taken a decade earlier. Stein sits with the paraphernalia of writing: weighty tomes on her desk, a pen in her hand, her paper in front of her, and her face obscured; her form is in shadow and only her hands, writing, are illuminated. Gertrude is in the foreground, Alice in the background, too far away for her expression to be made out; but Alice is surrounded by light, and Gertrude in the darkness. It seems to relay into one image the writerly isolation that Stein had lived with since *The Making of Americans*, as well as Alice's viewpoint throughout the book; on the threshold, looking in. Both women are represented, and both are effaced.

The first readers of the book were shocked by its lucidity, having been made to believe that Stein was unintelligible. This was a jolly, readable, entertaining jape of a book. It did indeed become the bestseller that turned the cult figure into a fully fledged celebrity. It did, as she wanted it to do, fix her public image, despite the elaborate rhetorical absenting of herself. Later she said that she had told all she wanted to tell about her life in her autobiographies; she felt that readers could find out anything they wanted to know about her, the answers to all their questions, from her books. She wanted her legend to stand as she had made it. As Janet Flanner wrote: 'She thought she had no personality aside from her writing.'[33]

The book also dislodged popular notions of her as an ivory tower-dweller. As one of her biographers, Janet Hobhouse put it:

'The American public fell in love with the character of Gertrude Stein, like Victorian readers with Little Nell.'[34] In 1934 the French edition also made her a celebrity there. She was a 60-year-old debutante, emerging from obscurity.

She was more serious, of course, than the success of her most popular book, a humorous book, allowed her to be seen as. It was indeed almost as though she had revealed a double personality, which is why she wrote *Stanzas in Meditation*, in her other style.[35] *Stanzas in Meditation* is a parallel text for the *Autobiography*, and could not be more different from it. It was written at the same time and takes as its subject Stein's apprehensiveness about the venture she was embarked on. In this work she agonised over what she was doing – writing plainly – and wished people would listen instead to the 'real' her. In *Stanzas in Meditation* Stein acknowledged the worrying interchangeableness of her own and Alice's authorial personae when she wrote: 'I have often thought that she meant what I said.'[36] She also made one of the first uses of what would become one of her mythical refrains: 'What is the difference if there is no question and no answer[?]'[37] The question and answer structure had been part of those playful early compositions in which Alice became interrogator and answerer, and their roles intertwined. That 'double personality' was also what enabled her to say, in *Everybody's Autobiography*, that she discovered in writing autobiography that you 'could not be yourself because you cannot remember right . . . you are of course never yourself'[38] – a typically sceptical, Steinian statement. That doubleness has since become an easy cliché in terms of her reception; that there was the writing that could be read, and the writing that could not be read, the easy, charming and loveable Stein, and the difficult, subversive and untrustworthy one.[39]

She was getting a lot of fan mail from American readers. The opening of *Four Saints in Three Acts* had taken place in New York. Virgil Thomson, who had commissioned the piece from her and

Four Saints in Three Acts, 1934.

written the score, was in charge of the production. Partly cashing in on the trend for 'exoticism' that had grabbed white New Yorkers since the Harlem Renaissance (which Stein's friend Carl Van Vechten had played a role in), it was Thomson's idea to have an all-black cast. The result was a sensation. On the opening night Van Vechten wrote to Stein that he hadn't seen an audience more excited since the *Rite of Spring* (where his path had first crossed Stein's). 'The difference', he added, 'was that they were pleasurably excited.' Toscanini was there applauding.[40] Her friends wrote to her telling her to come to America and lap up the glory. Gertrude and Alice bought a new set of clothes each – Gertrude sported a new line in trim, business-like suits, and a leopard-skin hat. Stein, who throughout her Paris years had always insisted on how American she was, was to return to the USA after a thirty-year absence. According to biographer Linda Wagner-Martin, while Alice was fearful of the homophobia they might face, Stein was more concerned about possible anti-Semitism.[41] In the end neither of their fears were founded, and none of their preconceptions could not have prepared them for their incredible reception.

When their ship got to New York on 24 October 1934 there was a boatful of reporters and photographers waiting to greet them. The journalists bombarded her with questions. When they asked her 'why don't you write the way you talk?' she shot back: 'why don't you read the way I write?' They delighted in branding her 'The Sibyl of Montparnasse'. The lights in Times Square announced: 'Gertrude Stein has arrived in New York'; 'As if we did not know it', said Alice. The next week in *The New Yorker* there was a cartoon of a customs inspector saying: 'Gertrude says four hats is a hat is a hat.'[42] A Pathé newsreel was made of Stein being interviewed. Van Vechten organized a party for Stein and Toklas in New York, at which George Gershwin played. Stein was everywhere: on the radio, in the papers, and making personal appearances on a whistle-stop, sell-out lecture tour of the country, from New York and Chicago first, to Yale, Bryn Mawr and Harvard, then to Wisconsin, Minnesota, Michigan, Ohio, Indiana and on to Virginia, Louisiana and Texas, lecturing, taking classes at universities and meeting fans: all orchestrated by Alice, who, as they toured the country, was referred to as Stein's 'secretary' or 'travelling companion'. (Even in most personal memoirs written about the period in which the couple appear, she was simply Stein's 'friend'.) Stein was front-page news wherever she went. Alice was oddly unobtrusive. The media hardly noticed this ever-present alter ego walking in Miss Stein's shadow, even though the book had been written in her name.

Stein understood the importance of becoming a personality in order to make money from her work, having seen her friends and protégés do the same. So she agreed to being carted around on a precursor of the modern celebrity book tour: in style – she was a national heroine. She was startled by the advances of the machine

The window of Gimbel Brothers' department store, New York, photographed by
Carl Van Vechten, 1934.

age in America, particularly the amount of electric light, but told
Natalie Barney that she was able to cross the street in New York
with impunity because even the taxi drivers 'recognise me and are
careful of me'[43] – a sign of her unshakeable faith in the power of
her own image. She was received at the White House and met
Franklin and Eleanor Roosevelt, neither of whom impressed her.
She visited Hollywood, where she had a natural affinity for the
Californian stars, and for the literary celebrities of her home country, some of whom she already knew from Paris. At one dinner
party Anita Loos, Charlie Chaplin, Dashiell Hammett and Lillian
Hellman were all in attendance. She had chosen the guests herself,
and had been particularly keen to meet Hammett, with whom she
spoke about her love of detective novels, and what she saw as the
unimaginative way in which male writers wrote about men, which
she put down to a crisis in masculine confidence.[44] On a live prime-
time radio interview for NBC, Bennett Cerf, the president of
Random House, said: 'I'm very proud to be your publisher, Miss

Stein, but as I've always told you, I don't understand very much of what you're saying.' To which she replied: 'Well, I've always told you, Bennett, you're a very nice boy but you're rather stupid.'[45]

Stein was never afraid to mix her love of the lowbrow with her high modernism. She upbraided Sylvia Beach for not stocking certain pulp writers in her very high-minded bookshop, and claimed to read one detective novel a day. In the USA she became obsessively interested in the language of advertisements, particularly the Burma-Shave commercials with their punning billboard rhymes. By this stage of her life Stein wore her learning lightly, and she sometimes succeeded in deceiving people into thinking that she was something of an idiot savant. She had spent a lifetime being mocked, and she had her own vindication. But it was a dangerous game which impaired her reputation.

Her reaction to celebrity was to take it on as a sort of role play, a game. Even down to publicizing her insistence that she would 'only' lecture to 500 people at a time, which supposed exclusivity made her lectures more popular and ensured they were over-subscribed. Bennett Cerf later eulogized her as 'the publicity hound of the world – simply great; she could have been a tremendous hit in show business'.[46] But she dumped her agent, William Aspenwall Bradley, because he was too commercial, explaining to Carl Van Vechten (who was busy delightedly organizing parties to receive her everywhere she went): 'There are some things a girl cannot do.'[47]

Although it clearly pandered to her megalomaniac tendencies, fame also disturbed her. Having a readership was a more difficult and painful thing than Stein could have imagined. In *The Making of Americans* she had expressed her doubts that she would ever even have a reader, but now it had made her doubt herself.

Stein was one of the first subjects of the burgeoning phenomenon of literary celebrity at a time when modern celebrity in general was changing. Fame no longer had the same value or meant the same that it had, and pop culture was on the horizon. The ability

Gertrude and Alice on the radio, 1934.

to drive the publicity machine was now becoming the most important factor in achieving celebrity.[48] Stein's connection with this false celebrity did her as much harm as good. That her image actually detracted from her writing made her telling of her own life more problematic. It has made criticism of her work and speculation about her life eternally intertwined; she herself was presented with these problems and confronted them in her writing. In her lectures she addressed in detail the differences publicity, broadcasting and what she saw as the newspaper mentality were making to literary expression – not just her own – in America.

She wrote that it was 'upsetting' to see her name in lights; when she saw herself on the newsreel she was unnerved; and the night before her first lecture she had to call a doctor because her throat was so constricted she couldn't speak.[49] It was a combination of

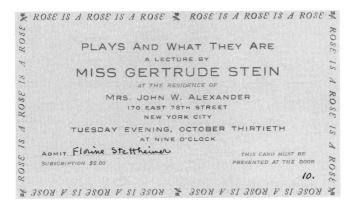

Florine Stettheimer's invitation to hear her fellow hostess speak.

being stagestruck and a deeper anxiety, a vacancy that she had discovered in the midst of adulation. And it made her lose her voice in
another important way too. In 1933–4 she stopped writing for the
first time in thirty years. Stein was a strenuous writer, a writer of
enormous stamina – but she was brought to wordlessness by fame,
by suddenly having a readership, a 'buyer'.[50] She admitted that it
made her 'nervous'. It becomes clear, from reading the subversions
of her own straightforwardness in *Stanzas in Meditation* and
Everybody's Autobiography, that *The Autobiography of Alice B. Toklas*
was practically a piece of self-exploitation, so traumatic was it in
the writing and its repercussions, for Stein.

But her lectures and university appearances were a great success.
Back in Boston, they called her 'Radcliffe's most famous daughter'.[51]
In these lectures, later published as *Lectures in America*, she addressed her audience as the genius she had proclaimed herself to
be, and rather than capitalizing on *The Autobiography*, took it as
an opportunity to deliver her thoughts on serious questions such
as 'What Are Masterpieces and Why Are There so Few of Them?',
and 'What is English Literature?', which she went at in her usual
sidelong manner. Often it was as though she had to plead with or

cajole her audience into understanding her: 'Oh yes you do see./ You do see that.'[52] It is uncertain whether this was down to self-doubt – doubt about her own ability to make herself understood – or doubt of her audience's capacity for understanding her. (In Radcliffe, faced with the po-faced women she had distrusted since her time there, she changed her pleas for her audience to understand to a curt: 'Maybe you will, but I doubt it.'[53]) She wrote her lectures in one of her 'difficult' styles, and in fact offered few concessions to ease understanding. Nevertheless there was a similar sense of demystification to that she had engendered in Oxford in 1926, because of the informal question and answer sessions that invariably followed them. In Chicago, she gave her famous explanation of the rose line:

> I notice that you all know it: you make fun of it, but you know it. Now listen! I'm no fool. I know that in daily life we don't go round saying 'is a . . . is a . . . is a . . .'. Yes, I'm no fool, but I think that in that line the rose is red for the first time in English poetry for a hundred years.[54]

When she talked off the cuff, as Bennett Cerf put it: 'she talked as plain as a banker'.[55]

This was the Depression, and having written a gloriously upbeat memoir about a community of mischievous artists that seemed to celebrate frivolity, for the newspapers Stein was the light relief. Her own life, and the lives she wrote about that intersected her own in *The Autobiography*, were the celebrity lives that represented a distraction from the grinding hardships being faced by many of her readers. Inevitably there were those who found her distasteful. Isaac Goldberg wrote admonishingly of her in 1934: 'an expatriate American, writing a language all but hermetic, poles removed from the common people and from their problems and interests, addicted to snobbery (the *Alice B. Toklas* is one of the most snobbish documents printed in this century, and perhaps in any other), suddenly is catapulted into the democracy of popularity. And she loves it.'[56] This was strong criticism, but also epitomized critical bafflement about where to place Stein. That licence that Stein had given to those who populated her microcosm of bohemia, her flagrantly apolitical stories of artists doing as they pleased, for many did not sit well with the times. Her own seriousness, in fact, sits uneasily with the figure she had become. By 1933 she had already nurtured two generations of writers, but in October 1934 she was the laughing stock of *The New Yorker*'s Talk of the Town column – even down to her underwear.

After the American lecture tour Random House had offered to publish one book of hers a year, to which she responded with eager incredulity. Despite the enterprise of Plain Edition, Stein had never gone solo in her publishing efforts by choice, or to strike out as an avant-garde, but only by necessity – *Tender Buttons* was the first thing of hers anyone else agreed to publish, and that was ten years after she had started writing. Then it wasn't until *Useful Knowledge* in 1928 – another fourteen years – that any mainstream publisher would touch her work, or want to pay for it.[57]

In *The Autobiography* she complained about how unadventurous the large publishing houses were – but she desperately wanted the money and acclaim that she thought they could bring her. Small print runs and inadequate distribution dogged her print career. She was hoping, as she had with her lectures, to use her celebrity as a way of getting people to read her other work. It did help her to achieve a wider circulation, but she also shot herself in the foot. She riled people into making more and more ridiculous parodies. The other stuff was not easy enough – it wasn't what people wanted. Later Alice recounted the story of how James Branch Cabell, sitting next to her at a dinner party, leant over conspiratorially and asked: 'Is Gertrude Stein serious?' Alice's answer was concise: 'Desperately', she replied. 'That puts a different light on it', said the writer.[58]

In May 1935 Stein and Toklas set sail again for France. The story of what had happened on her triumphant return to America, during the Depression, is told in the second of her autobiographies, *Everybody's Autobiography*. It is both a sequel and a response to her first autobiography, and a full reading of it is somewhat dependent on having read *Alice B. Toklas*. *Everybody's Autobiography* could be seen as even more a commercial stunt; it clearly traded on the first autobiography's popularity; the name-dropping was still there – but there was a change. It is a fascinating book: a serious writer writing about fame from her own point of view as a personality, having gained a celebrity completely unrelated to her serious writing, her life's work – perhaps a paradox unrepeated anywhere else in literary history. In *Everybody's Autobiography* Stein reclaimed her indirect style. There is an undermining, puzzling technique at work as she redoes scenes from *The Autobiography* in a voice that felt truer to herself: more sceptical. It was a continuation of the story in Hollywood and the reception of the former autobiography, and how it affected her. Calling it *Everybody's Autobiography* was a stretch, but it was a nod to her identity being in the public domain.

Stein had deliberately put autobiography to the same purpose as publicity, without compunction or false feelings about authorial truth. She had a disdain for pretending it was 'true'. In *Everybody's Autobiography* she said it was impossible to 'remember right'; her whole writing career had been about a similar inability, so she was hardly likely to pretend otherwise now. But after celebrity, she had to become a new kind of autobiographer. In the introduction she wrote that 'anything is an autobiography'. 'Alice B. Toklas did hers and now anybody will do theirs', and Stein, wresting back her story from 'Alice's' clutches, becomes a sort of everyman.[59] Her first autobiography had been emptied of her own discourse. *Alice B. Toklas* was self-advertisement. Now she would begin to address once again how to really write about herself. This included oppressive thoughts about death, and connectedly, the book records her displeasure at being told (very early on, by her brother Leo) that it was her personality people were interested in, not her work. 'Identity always worries me and memory and eternity.'[60]

She had been in 1937 to London, where she had been snapped by Cecil Beaton, and had more parties thrown for her, pursuing her fame in British literary circles, in a watered-down version of her American success. Just as she had found seeing her name in lights 'upsetting', she found the triumphant London staging of *A Wedding Bouquet*, a ballet based on one of her plays, disconcerting; she felt, staring out into the darkness of the auditorium taking her bows, that it had nothing to do with her. Stein's anxiety stemmed from the separation of her public image from her work. In her treatment of time in *Everybody's Autobiography* once again she was at home with her insistence on the present moment, as a way of overcoming that distance and despair. Rather than optimism, this was what Bridgman calls her 'pessimistic stoicism'.[61]

Partly because of the smokescreen of self-conscious naivety in *The Autobiography*, and partly because of her instinctive reaction that if a readership was not available the next best thing was a public, Stein's work and her image got horribly interlocked. Stein's image was about the whole product, the display, the element of performance. Whereas once writing had been a private act, now she made a pose of writing in public places; *Lucy Church Amiably* was composed outdoors; she wanted it to be like a landscape, so, like a painter, she went and sat in the landscape in order to absorb it. She listened to acoustic patterns to get the thread of a piece. She wrote to the noise of a tap dripping; she wrote in the car (for example, she wrote 'Composition as Explanation', her complex exegesis of her own style, in a garage while someone was fixing her car). The car itself, the source of much hilarity and hi-jinks, was like the poodle, another prop. When she stood and took her bows on the London stage she realized that the writer had become the image, the act, and it upset her, because it seemed to foretell how literary history

Gertrude Stein as a puppet in *Identity* by Donald Vestal, Detroit Institute of Arts, 1936.

was already summing her up. That she wrote about these issues and made them the focus of her art made the boundaries even less clear. This confusion of subject matter is also one of the things that has made Stein criticism so bound up with biography.

Evidently concerned about her own misrepresentation, she entered her period of explaining her own work. In *Lectures in America* and *Narration* (the published title of four more lectures delivered in 1935 in Chicago) she began explaining how she wrote in such deceptively simple-sounding titles as 'How Writing is Written', or 'Poetry and Grammar', where she invented a comic snobbery about punctuation: 'I could never bring myself to use a question mark'; commas were servile and the use of them was 'positively degrading'.[62] In *The Autobiography* itself she had defensively written: 'Gertrude Stein, in her writing, has always been possessed by the intellectual passion for exactitude in the description of inner and outer reality.'[63] Her writing had become full of defences of her style, and herself.

In *Lectures in America* she now called Wells, Galsworthy, Bennett – the very men to whom she had hopefully sent *Three Lives* a quarter of a century earlier – the 'second-class' writers. She claimed that literature had needed to move out of the nineteenth century, and it was the USA that had taken it into the twentieth century. It was she, an American woman, who had naturally been at the forefront of such a mission.[64] The freedom to use words as she liked; she saw this as an American condition. The America she had seen left a lasting impression on her, and on her return to Paris she turned once again to patriotic themes, in 'What America Means to Me', *The Geographical History of America*, and *Four in America*. In these pieces she also continued to write about the problem of identity, and reputation. *Four in America* imagines – erratically – what would have happened if George Washington had been a novelist, Henry James a general, Wilbur Wright a painter and Ulysses S. Grant a religious leader. And in *Four in America* she decided that 'I am I because my little dog knows me' (which had been one of her repetitive slogans) is a false proposition; she could no longer believe that her existence or identity depended on the world's view of her.

During her 1937 visit to London for the opening of *A Wedding Bouquet* she had been startled by the publicity surrounding Wallis Simpson. When Stein had lived in Baltimore at 215 East Biddle Street forty years earlier, Wallis Warfield, later Simpson, lived opposite at number 212. Struck by the coincidence of the fame each of them had recently achieved, as much as their enormous differences, Stein decided to write a novel on the subject of her former neighbour. *Ida, a Novel* would be published in 1940. It was about identity, and had a central character, Ida, who was both idle and an idol, and who was mainly interested in shopping. It was a droll book, and had its moments of black humour. She sent a copy to Mrs Simpson, who thanked her and hoped one day to be able to understand it.

Endlessly inventive in her prose and in her life she moved seamlessly into new incarnations. She drifted away from influence over modern painters – all that had faded. But her writing was at least now more read. And still the younger writers kept coming; Henry Miller, for example, sent her *Tropic of Cancer* asking for advice. Apart from the continuing adventures in autobiography, the experiment did not ease up. Having overcome her writer's block, Stein was becoming as prolific as she had ever been. Between 1936 and 1940 she wrote several children's stories, in which familiar themes were apparent: 'Once upon a time I met myself and ran' is a startling refrain from *The World is Round*. She wrote another libretto, *Doctor Faustus Lights the Lights* in 1938 (first produced 1951), her enigmatic version of the Faust legend.

All these writings are full of 'pessimistic stoicism'; there was undoubtedly a darkness creeping into her work. Perhaps it was the sobering threat of impending war that made Stein also start to see the value of revision at this stage, an idea of final versions, final days, final statements. There was a Laurence Sternian ending to her philosophical meditation on the relation of human nature to the human mind, *The Geographical History of America*: 'I am not sure that is not the end.'[65] It was very far from being the end.

Eight

Stein appears to have been completely unsentimental about having to relinquish the scene of her decades of glory. In 1938 she was forced to leave 27 rue de Fleurus, as the landlord needed the apartment for his son. Stein and Toklas moved to the rue Christine, a street with its own illustrious ghosts; their new flat was in the building where Queen Christina of Sweden had once lived, and which their old friend Apollinaire had written about in 'Lundi, rue Christine'. While Stein and Toklas were moving house, others were fleeing Paris, and France. By December 1939 her American friends were warning her to leave. They encouraged her to come back to the USA, where she was now famous, and had many friends, but she decided to stay put. She and Toklas put their papers in order, then went back to their country house at Bilignin in southeastern France, taking the Picasso *Portrait of Gertrude Stein* with them. (They had already sent many of Stein's papers to Yale for safe-keeping.) They would not return to Paris until December 1944.

When the Second World War arrived Stein was in her sixties. Stein and Toklas, both Jewish, lived in rural France under German occupation, where Stein continued to write, and produced several books about the war. German soldiers were even billeted in their house during August and September 1943, and again in July 1944 German soldiers came and stayed for the night. The pair kept out of the way and allowed the servants to see to the soldiers' needs.

Theirs was a precarious situation. To what they owed their miraculous survival has been a point of contention.

They had repeatedly been told by the American consul in Lyon to leave while they could. In early June 1940 they were packed and ready to go; but then they made the decision not to leave. Stein explained it with her ordinary, somewhat bombastic good cheer: 'it would be awfully uncomfortable and I am fussy about my food.'[1] When she retold the story in *Wars I Have Seen*, she made it into a reassuring tale of neighborly solidarity; the villagers had promised that they would look after them, '*en famille*',[2] so that they felt happier staying where they were, rather than going to live among strangers, even when Paris fell to the Germans.

The region where they lived became part of the Vichy government, and at first German troops were removed from the area. In 'The Winner Loses' (August 1940) Stein hoped that, staying where they were, they would be 'tremendously occupied with the business of daily living, and that will be enough.'[3] Stein read the classics, and books of astrological predictions and prophecies. They did everything to supplement their meagre supplies, from fishing for crayfish with an umbrella to working the black market, and Gertrude would go out foraging, walking miles every day for a few eggs, some milk. While Gertrude's famous charm came in very useful, her international renown also naturally made them extremely conspicuous. In 1943, their money running out, they made the journey to Switzerland in order to sell Cézanne's *Portrait of Madame Cézanne*, and the perilous return journey back into France; after which Stein commented: 'we are eating the Cézanne'.[4] Her instinct was to turn everything into anecdote, even if it was a lugubrious one. Her friends asked why they had come back.

According to Toklas, they simply 'refused to face' the danger that faced them as Jews, and when the US entered the war, as Americans.[5] In 1943 Stein, drawing unnecessary attention to

Stein's identity papers.

herself, brought a lawsuit against the owner of their house at Bilignin who was forcing them to move, and one day when she went to see her lawyer he informed her that he had been told directly by a Vichy official that Stein and Toklas must leave at once, 'otherwise they will be put into a concentration camp'.[6] Again, plans for escape were made and again Stein and Toklas turned back at the last minute. Stein decided 'it is better to go regularly wherever we are sent than to go irregularly where nobody can help us if we are in trouble.'[7] Stein later wrote that the mayor had told her, when enemy aliens were being rounded up by German soldiers, that she and Alice were too old to be sent to a concentration camp and would not survive it, so he did not tell anyone about them. They were not made to sign the register of Jewish residents at Culoz.[8] Having friends in high places had never been so important.

Stein's story of being protected by the kind-hearted villagers was appealing, but it was only part of the truth, and the reasons for Gertrude and Alice's survival are still somewhat obscure. Francis Rose, a protégé of Jean Cocteau, one of the second-rate painters Stein had latched onto before the war (she was rumoured to have bought 400 of his works) and who would eventually design her gravestone, was also an intimate of several senior Nazi figures. He claimed to have asked Goering to ensure the safety of Stein and Toklas. More controversial still is Stein's relationship with her pre-war friend Bernard Faÿ, he who had translated *The Making of Americans*, 'Melanctha' and *The Autobiography* into French.[9] Faÿ was given a position as head of the Bibliothèque Nationale by the Vichy government, and it was probably due to his influence with high-ranking Vichy officials that their names did not appear on any lists of Jewish residents, and that Gertrude and Alice were safe during the war.

Naturally they were grateful to him. It seems that they were unaware of the darker side of his wartime activities. In 1944 Faÿ was arrested for collaborating and at his trial in 1946 was sentenced to hard labour for life, later reduced to twenty years. Gertrude wrote a long testimonial on his behalf, wrote to him in prison and sent him gifts. After Stein's death, Alice Toklas devoted much of her time to campaigning for his release. When they first met Faÿ must have seemed just another of the harmless, sycophantic, slightly ridiculous if useful young men who flocked around Stein. But events proved that he was not harmless. Janet Malcolm has recently uncovered more about Bernard Faÿ. She writes on evidence from his trial that he 'was responsible for many deaths', and that '540 Freemasons were shot or died in the camps' as a result of his collaboration.[10] It is not suggested that Stein or Toklas knew anything about this. Nevertheless Stein's deep bond of affection for Faÿ, unperturbed by his post-war arrest, raises questions about her judgement. That he also may have saved her life makes the matter more complex.

Relatedly, another stain on Stein's reputation has been caused by her championing of Marshal Pétain, the head of the Vichy government, for the selfish reason that under the terms of the Armistice the unoccupied area of France in which they lived had felt to her 'pretty free', as opposed to 'not free at all' if they had been occupied;[11] she saw Pétain as their personal saviour, but she was much vilified for this after the war, as she has continued to be more recently by critics and biographers measuring up her politics. It would not have been so bad if Stein had not became a propagandist for Pétain, translating his speeches into English during 1941 and 1942 and writing an effusive preface for them. Bernard Faÿ met Pétain at Vichy on a monthly basis, and would often travel to visit Stein and Toklas after those meetings. Stein was clearly under his influence, and it was probably at his suggestion that she began the translation. A blend of political ignorance and personal gratitude led her to sing Pétain's praises. But she continued with the translation even after it was known that Jews were being deported.[12] Her American publisher referred to the translation as a 'disgusting' document.

After the war, Stein was even suspected by some former friends of having collaborated; Maria Jolas stated as much. The allegations were unfounded, but questions over her behaviour and opinions have lingered and infected her posthumous reputation. Katherine Anne Porter also criticized Stein's stance during the war, objecting to what she saw as her attitude that it was all a bit of a wheeze. Stein could often sound flippant when she was in reality anything but. After reporting the conversation about the concentration camp in *Wars I Have Seen*, for example, she writes: 'It took us some weeks to get over it but we finally did.'[13] Of course Stein was not underestimating the seriousness of the situation; she was however bound by a lifetime's habit of putting a cheerful face on everything. When they got back to Paris after the war she castigated Alice for bemoaning the fact that their apartment had been looted of knick-knacks, telling her their problems had been trifling compared to those faced by others.

She had in fact made an abrupt about-turn with the Pétain speeches, and abandoned the translation. Although apparently having written it for publication in America as an apologia for Pétain, Stein appears to have reconsidered. Later she revised her opinion of Pétain, extenuating herself with an element of obfuscation, admitting her own ultimate confusion as well as the complexity of the situation, by saying: 'So many points of view about him, so very many, I had lots of them, I was almost French in having so many'.[14]

Despite the many petty quarrels that Stein was renowned for during her life, she can be both admirable and exasperating in the breadth of her philosophical tolerance. To Cecil Beaton she once explained: 'I can't put up with anyone who has set ideas, with any-one who is *parti pris*.'[15] That breadth of philosophical tolerance is in most contexts one of her most appealing characteristics. In a letter to Francis Rose she simply said: 'living in an occupied country is very complicated.'[16] Stein could be infuriatingly open-minded. Her arguments were never watertight, and it was almost as if she never meant them to be.

The older Stein made a series of ill-advised comments on the political situation that gave her a reputation as a reactionary. In the 1930s she opposed Roosevelt and his New Deal, seemed to lend support to Franco, and gushed over Pétain, all of which earned her detractors. Many have been disappointed and mystified that Stein should espouse right-wing solutions to economic and political problems; her lesbianism and her avant-gardism seem to make her a natural ally of those with Leftist sympathies, and people have found it hard to believe that she was simply not to be corralled under any unifying belief system, or that one person could be so radical and so conservative at once. In fact, she had always been a conservative; her first novella had extolled the virtues of being middle class and living temperately. Critics have been disappointed in her for her failure to live up to the meanings with which they have loaded her.

During the war Stein and Toklas were clearly frightened. Two Jewish American women in their sixties living alone in occupied France would have been hard pressed not to be. Biographer Janet Hobhouse put the fact that they decided to stay down to 'childishness' rather than 'courage'. Stein has been seen as not identifying enough with her Jewish heritage.[17] It is very hard to make such judgements. If any of her comments seem crass, they are clearly also a front. Stein was never one to give a typical reaction. Her lifelong attitude to adversity was optimism, but it was in her writing that her true feelings were played out. For the first time in her work of the period she began to address the depression of her youth.

Stein's war writing, as unconventional as any of her other work, begins with *Paris France* (in fact written before war broke out), known as Stein's 'love letter' to France. It is not really about Paris, but about rural France and the people among whom she lived. It begins with some barely optimistic comments about civilization and progress. Here she told herself, managing composure on the brink of apocalypse, that she had to be 'completely conservative' 'in order to be free'.[18]

Once the occupation began, Stein continued writing, but in her barely intelligible scrawl; Alice no longer typed any of it up, so that German soldiers would not be able to read it if they got hold of it. In public they had to speak in French and not English, a circumstance that made her more patriotic than ever about her language. Stein was still being published, in the journal *Confluences*, until her name appeared on a Nazi list of proscribed authors in May 1943. Local children performed the plays she wrote for them – words by Gertrude Stein, costumes by Pierre Balmain – plays full of signs and portents.[19] The war was taking her back to her democratic roots. She had always objected to her plays being performed in an elitist setting, and this was, in the best way, art for the people. In one of the plays, perhaps her best, 'Yes is For a Very Young Man', Stein explores the ideology of saying yes and no, of assent and dissent, and of affirmation and negation: 'What is there to say but yes, no does not mean anything.' The piece has been read as evidence of Stein's involvement in the Resistance; there is the possibility, but no proof, that she was providing information to the Resistance during these years.[20]

The plays and other pieces that she was producing are not doctrinal or dogmatic; rather they are filled with surrealistic moments, dramas, tensions, little sinister, unexplained tableaux that seek to represent the psychological confusion of those years. In her epilogue to *Mrs Reynolds*, the peculiar allegory she wrote about Hitler and Stalin between 1940 and 1942, she wrote: 'There is nothing historical about this book except the state of mind.'[21] That is a good dictum for Stein's war writing, in which history becomes a state of mind. During the war Stein read books of prophecy for solace, and *Mrs Reynolds* is full of dreams and signs, but also about the unexceptional nature of day to day life in the occupation, a tribute to unexceptional things; it celebrates contentment, but not unthinkingly: it is a hard-won contentment, in spite of hardship. Battling with horror internally, it faces the world with equanimity.

The most successful of her war writings, *Wars I Have Seen* was written, a diary of sorts, between early 1943 and August 1944, when the American troops arrived. It is her chronicle of the last stage of the war. Here the themes of the war years came together, though chaotically; here Stein described a world in which chaos and coincidence ruled, and there was no possibility of progress; no facts could explain the situation; realism was dead. *Wars I Have Seen* was, perhaps, based on her old friend Mildred Aldrich's World War I book of letters, *A Hilltop on the Marne*, in which Aldrich, at the time in her sixties, recorded the everyday experience of living in wartime, in a house which overlooked the plains on which the battles of the Marne took place. Stein, subsisting on the edge and under the weight of another world war, now also in her sixties, was like Aldrich reporting the mundane and the trivial side of war, although in her very un-mundane manner. *Wars I Have Seen* also records the divided loyalties of life under occupation, the turning of villager against villager, as some were denounced to officials for dealing on the black market, and the Maquis sent little coffins to those accused of collaboration. One of her alternative titles for it was 'An Emotional Autobiography'.

The last stages of the book, dealing with the liberation, are practically euphoric. When the first Americans arrived in the local town, she rushed to meet them: 'Alice Toklas panting behind and Basket very excited', as she put it, with a rather unflattering reversal of roles for Alice and the dog.[22] *Wars I Have Seen* was a popular and critical success when it was published in 1945.

After the war, Stein learned that in August 1944 the Gestapo had been in her apartment in the rue Christine, carrying a photograph of her, calling her Picasso paintings '*la saloperie juive*' and threatening to burn them.[23] In war writing such as *Wars I have Seen* Stein had been forced to set aside her autocratic tendencies and see herself as part of history. The war had changed her. During the occupation, Stein was forced to live in the present, and among people again; she could no longer isolate herself, and she went at her work with a new and less cavalier engagement in public affairs.

Aged 71, she was in fine shape as a writer. In liberated Paris Stein became a maternal figure for American GIs as she entertained them and listened to their stories. Yet another generation of young men was falling for her. She told Cecil Beaton that the GIs came to see her and Picasso because they recognized that they too were fighters.[24] Her image was still as famous as ever – to promote *Wars I Have Seen* a photograph of Stein and Toklas appeared in response to a glamorous publicity photo of Kathleen Winsor, the author of

Feeding the GIs.

Forever Amber, with the line: 'Shucks, we've got glamour girls too', which greatly amused her.[25] The war over, in June 1945 she embarked, under the auspices of *Life* magazine, on a tour of US army bases in occupied Germany, bringing food and chatting with GIs. Stein wrote a piece about it with the sprightly title 'Off We All Went to See Germany', and it appeared with a spread of photographs of herself and Alice on the roof of Hitler's Berghof at Berchtesgaden (she had wanted to steal one of Hitler's radiators to grow flowers over, but found it too heavy to appropriate). She was still as concerned as ever to disseminate serenely triumphant images of herself.

And she turned once more to America. *Brewsie and Willie* is an extraordinary emulation of dialogue between the GIs she met on her tour and in Paris. It recreates conversations between American soldiers and nurses, about the future of America, demonstrating again Stein's skill at emulating vernaculars. She had always used dialogue and conversation in her work, from 'Melanctha' onwards, partly as a way of remaining indefinite, exploring contradictoriness. The appeal of dialogue was also that it did not involve argument; Stein was not a practitioner of the prolonged argument. But with some polemic fervour, *Brewsie and Willie* launched a critique of what Stein saw as the spoilt American culture, from mushy food to the newly invented Gallup poll, which aroused her perennial objection to the idea of being expected to answer a simple yes or no to anything, and railed against the evils of industrialism in America.

The book was a call for individualism, and a reminder that Stein was always not only an autocrat, but an individualist. 'How can you pioneer when there ain't no wilderness any more' asks Brewsie. The nurse responds: 'you got to break down what's been built up, that's pioneering.'[26] A fair enough summing up of Stein's artistic goals, which were always linked to her vision for America, and an American twentieth century. One of the most characteristic lines in the book is: 'There ain't any answer . . . that's the answer.' Stein's fundamental incapability of furnishing 'an answer' in her work, at the very root of her style, was related to her view of the world. At the end of what was to be Stein's last book, and the most unusual of her unusual war writings, the address 'To Americans' is a fairly startling farewell speech. The GIs had 'made me come over all patriotic.' As a valediction, it gives a strikingly different image of Stein to the one that had prospered in the public imagination, or even the one that has prospered since in the critical tradition that has sprung up around her work since the 1970s:

You just have to find a new way . . . you have to learn to produce without exhausting your country's wealth, you have to learn to be individual and not just mass job workers . . . you have to get courage enough to know what you feel and not just all be yes or no men, you have to really learn to express complication . . . look facts in the face, not just what they all say, the leaders, but every darn one of you . . . We are Americans.[27]

It is a reminder of the array of contexts that feed into the arc of her career that she called herself 'a Civil War veteran', and ended in the age of the atomic bomb.

Since the war Stein's understanding of the race problem in America had advanced; she wrote, in an article for the *New York Times*, that American soldiers were now beginning to understand what imprisonment and persecution meant, and because of that they were beginning to understand that the race problem in America was also about persecution and a sense of imprisonment.[28] She too had become conscious of the meaning of freedom. The war may also have made Stein, belatedly, into a feminist. *The Mother of Us All* (1946) was a libretto (again commissioned by Virgil Thomson, and first performed to his music in 1947) about the life of Susan B. Anthony, the nineteenth-century women's rights reformer and campaigner for female suffrage. It was a peculiar subject for Stein, who had never identified with female role models, and never aligned herself with any feminist ideologies, except that it treated a subject who was perhaps a Stein substitute. Anthony is a strong female figure who, in the end, reaches a sort of apotheosis. She is a great speaker. She is the type of the genius whose work stands above time. The play itself is filled with silences, and not with answers, it is anti-sentiment, and also quite anti-male. Its ending is bleak; the disembodied voice of Susan B. Anthony sounds out from behind a memorial statue of Susan B. Anthony; after having asked, much as Stein did during her lectures, 'do you know', and receiving silence and negation as the only response, the voice from behind the statue intones her final words: 'My long life, my long life.' If this was Stein's memorial to herself, it was an uncharacteristically muted one.

By the time Stein wrote this, the last full-length work she would ever write, she knew she was ill. She was in some pain from what was at first thought to be a bowel infection, and later turned out to be cancer. She had lost a lot of weight and had weakened. Still

A window display devoted to Stein, 1946.

dwelling on death and destruction, her 'Reflection on the Atomic Bomb' would be the last piece Stein ever wrote. She died on 27 July 1946, aged 72, while being operated on for the cancer. She was buried in Père Lachaise cemetery. Alice eventually joined her there, twenty years later.

Stein's final words have achieved the status of legend all on their own. They have an entry in *The Oxford Book of Literary Quotations*. As told by Toklas, Stein was lying bewildered on a hospital bed, when she looked at Alice and asked her: 'what is the answer?' When Alice was silent, Gertrude continued: 'Well, in that case, what is the question?'[29] Perfect as this is, it has the ring of wishful invention. Alice's elegant hand is in it. Alice was still controlling the image, up until the last hours and beyond. Stein had played with various versions of this construction in her writing. She had given versions of her 'dying words' in *Everybody's Autobiography*,

'Sentences and Grammar' in *How to Write*, and *Brewsie and Willie*, as well as to reporters on board ship when she docked in New York. If these were her dying words, Stein was quoting herself. In the years that followed Alice would continue to exert as firm a grip as she was able on all interpretations of Stein. She devoted herself to bringing all the unpublished manuscripts into the light, policing the biography, guarding the portrait, polishing the legend.

As Janet Flanner put it: 'Gertrude Stein did not like questions and answers. She thought one should get answers without questions.'[30] She showed her disdain for a standard author questionnaire sent to her by the *Little Review*, with such responses as 'more of the same', when asked what she expected of the future, and 'I like to look at it', when they asked her what was her attitude to modern art. When reporters clambered aboard her ship in New York jostling for headline quotes, she responded to their questions with a far more interesting question of her own: 'Suppose no one asked a question. What would the answer be?'[31]

Her love of rhetoric and mannerism aligned her more with the books she had read in the British Museum as a young woman than with those of her own generation, the Elizabethan writers like John Lyly, passages from whose *Euphues* she had transcribed into her notebooks back in 1903. She recognized a devotion to antithesis and contradiction, a deliberate undermining of certainties, and it was in a euphuistic spirit that she set herself stylistic constrictions and patterns and rhetorical problems throughout her life. She had tetchily tried to convey the value of her idiosyncrasy, her pluralism, her Renaissance sensibility, to her American lecture audiences: '"The great trouble", she explained, "is that Americans have the idea that to understand something you must be able to immediately restate it."'[32] Stein took pleasure in open-endedness, in fact saw no other way to write or live.

She was the first to write her own life, almost incidentally becoming one of the century's great and groundbreaking autobiographers, and there have been many since. Numerous memoirs of that heady period on the Left Bank followed hers, and most of them paid her the homage of at least a mention. Biographies began appearing with Elizabeth Sprigge's, in 1957, which consulted Alice but of which Alice disapproved – and they continue to be written.

The papers reviewed her death using the same mixture of miscomprehension and bewildered bluster with which they had reviewed her work during life. Her obituarists praised the autobiography and suggested that the rest was nonsense, celebrated her charisma and her conversation, played up the relation with Picasso, Matisse and Hemingway. In the *New York Times* Toklas was described as 'her lifelong secretary-companion'.[33] Stein was bound for a long time in Wilson's idea of her as 'a literary personality'.[34] In the end her reputation rests on her life and personality as well as on her work, and the one reputation could not really exist without the other.

One opinion of *Wars I Have Seen* was of Stein's absorption in a word game while the world around her headed for catastrophe; 'a word game that assumes no responsibility'.[35] Even in the 1970s, the moral claims of Stein's work were still disputed. Janet Hobhouse wrote in her biography of Stein, *Everybody Who Was Anybody* (1975) that Stein's work is so extreme that it 'raises the question of whether writing has the right to make such demands'.[36] Such a question is implicit in the continuing marginality of much of her work, despite her fame. Perhaps no other writer has taken words to such extremes, or so flagrantly disregarded the demands of the reader, or the reader's comfort. But that charge of irresponsibility and irrelevance was surely not deserved.

She had very few sensible critics during her lifetime. By her death she was known for her one-liners, and was an easy reference point for all things avant garde. In the 1950s the eight-volume edition of the unpublished writings of Gertrude Stein was published, opening up a whole new cache of her serious writing.[37] In 1970

Red Grooms, *Gertrude*, 1975, colour lithograph and collage on paper mounted on paperboard.

Richard Bridgman's *Gertrude Stein in Pieces* gave Stein's readers a new narrative of her work; his explications, as much as his insistence that she was possible to explicate, lie behind much of Stein scholarship that followed. Meanwhile she was a hero for Beat poets; one should probably single out Lew Welch, who turned to writing after reading her work, and showed his gratitude in *How I Read Gertrude Stein*. Being a Californian, she was a special icon for the San Francisco Renaissance, both as an exponent of gay culture and of avant-garde writing. Her meanings proliferated as postmodernism grew, and in the 1970s her true glorification began, not just by biographers gilding the legend she bequeathed them, but by feminist and deconstructionist critics who found in her an early and abundantly rewarding figurehead. She was seen as part of a lineage of women writers providing an alternative to the masculine literary culture in which she worked. As many have pointed out, Stein devised her own 'literary theory' *avant la lettre*. As postmodern theory has fallen out of vogue, Stein has retained her stature, becoming other things to other readers. She is easily appropriated by factions.

Stein herself believed, insisted on pointing out, that she had been unfairly passed over, and that male modernists had taken the credit for many of her innovations. It is a moot point how far this was down to her gender, though it is true that she saw herself as occupying, and needing to occupy, a separate literary domain from her masculine contemporaries. Her misogyny has been well noted, but she wrote about women all her life and felt it necessary to state, late in her career in *The Geographical History of America* (referring of course to herself) that 'in this epoch the only real literary thinking has been done by a woman'.[38] What a boon she has been for feminist literary history.

She was normally elaborately genial, if insistent, about the subject, but on one occasion allowed herself a small rejoinder, when reporters continued to ask if she could really be serious: 'It's not our idea of fun to work for 30 or 40 years on a medium of expression and then have it ridiculed', she snapped.[39] Stein insisted on calling *The Making of Americans* 'the beginning of modern writing'.[40] She believed (or at least stated) that she, an American woman, was the embodiment of the creative force of the century, as if she herself had given birth to the modern era in her writing. She was one of the first writers who wrote with the consciousness that the reader could no longer trust the writer to provide a coherent narrative of the world, and included that consciousness within what she wrote, made it an essential part of what she wrote. She faced the world with a William Jamesian agnosticism, and a passionate, rigorous

Gertrude Stein with teleprinter, 1934.

individualism. In *Useful Knowledge* (another deliberately provocative title) she counted up to one hundred in the following manner: 'one and one and one and one and one and one . . .'.

Stein's true radical legacy lay in her insistence on showing how words and their meanings could be undone; she took it as her right that she had the freedom to use words exactly as she pleased, and in doing so she undermined the relation between words and the world, in the process flagging up the myriad problems – and perks – of describing consciousness using language. There are many reasons she was long consigned to irrelevance, not the least of which is her genuine difficulty but her work can also be a source of unique pleasure for the reader.[41] Janet Flanner remembered:

> A publisher once said to her, 'We want the comprehensible thing, the thing the public can understand.' She said to him: 'My work would have been no use to anyone if the public had understood me early and first.'[42]

Gertrude Stein in old age.

Perhaps it was because she was so fearful that she was always looking for praise. Her aphorism that 'nobody really lives who has not been well written about',[43] though it sounds like a cocktail party aperçu, is, baldly, a desperate statement. Her own life, as she wrote it, witticisms and all, became part of her work. She believed her 'personality' was her work. In *A Long Gay Book* Stein wrote that most people stop up their fear of death by procreation, by continuing themselves in another generation of flesh and blood.[44] Stein did it by writing – practically every day of her life from the age of 30 onwards. It was not wilfulness or thirst for celebrity that could make her continue experimenting in the face of ridicule and disinterest, from the 1890s to the 1940s: it was her obsession with language. Her peculiar eloquence resides in her belief that, as she wrote in a piece called 'Woodrow Wilson': 'Words are shocks.'[45] Her work is still extravagant in its strangeness. On her death there was already 'The Legend of Gertrude Stein', the legend of a life that intersected with the lives of hundreds of other writers and artists, the cultural creators of the twentieth century. She took her bows after the performance, and went back and pursued the perplexing, dark passageways of her difficult work.

As the fabled last words suggest, the important thing was never the answer, nor even the question. This succinct paradox became famous as Stein's dying communication because it so fittingly summed up her life and work. This was precisely the indeterminate area of philosophical speculation, in the very formation of thought, that her writing probed throughout her life. There is nothing final about it. Her work was an exploration of indeterminacy, an extraordinary thing for a writer to take as a lifetime's subject. Ever the provocateur, her final question, a questioning of all questions, is both mystical and humorous. It has the ring of a punchline – one can almost imagine Groucho Marx delivering it – and it is almost despairing, and almost resigned, but not quite: the hopeful wondering just about wins through. It's a happy thought to imagine that she retained that ambiguity until the end, which is deliberately not an ending. Stein's work, where it is comic, is seriously comic, in the way that her posing of that ultimate question, making it into her own last word, scripting her own death, is an epistemological jest: searching for that great twentieth-century white whale, authenticity, and knowing that it might not even exist.

References

Preface

1 Edmund Wilson, *The Shores of Light* (New York, 1952), p. 579.

One

1 Gertrude Stein, *Everybody's Autobiography* (New York, 1937), pp. 242–3.
2 Gertrude Stein, *Wars I Have Seen* (London, 1945), p. 8.
3 Quoted in Diana Souhami, *Gertrude and Alice* (London, 1991), p. 159.
4 Stein refers to the death of these siblings in *The Making of Americans* (Normal, IL, 1995), pp. 89, 796. This moment also surfaces elsewhere in Stein's work, for example in *Everybody's Autobiography*, pp. 115, 134.
5 Gertrude Stein, *Paris France* (London, 1940), p. 21.
6 Quoted in James R. Mellow, *Charmed Circle: Gertrude Stein and Company* (New York, 1974), p. 356.
7 Gertrude Stein, *Lectures in America* (New York, 1935), p. 150. Here Stein was quoting from her own *A Long Gay Book*.
8 Gertrude Stein to Robert Bartlett Haas, [23] January 1938, Yale Collection of American Literature, quoted in Brenda Wineapple, *Sister Brother: Gertrude and Leo Stein* (London, 1997), p. 61.
9 Gertrude Stein, *Brewsie and Willie* (New York, 1946), p. 113.
10 Stein, *The Making of Americans*, p. 3.
11 Ibid., p. 3.
12 Gertrude Stein, *Selected Writings of Gertrude Stein* (New York, 1972), p. 69.

13 Stein, *The Making of Americans*, p. 408.

14 Stein, *Everybody's Autobiography*, p. 132.

15 Stein, *The Making of Americans*, p. 3. These opening lines have provoked much comment. Stein is generally believed to have borrowed the story from Aristotle's *Nichomachean Ethics*.

16 Ibid., p. 125.

17 Ibid., p. 45.

18 Stein, *Lectures in America*, p. 66.

19 Stein, *Everybody's Autobiography*, pp. 135–7.

20 Mellow, *Charmed Circle*, p. 344.

21 William Carlos Williams, *The Autobiography of William Carlos Williams* (New York, 1951), p. 254.

22 Stein, *Selected Writings*, p. 71.

23 Gertrude Stein, 'The Birth of a Legend', in Rosalind S. Miller, *Gertrude Stein: Form and Intelligibility* (New York, 1949), p. 134.

24 Stein, *The Making of Americans*, p. 36.

25 Stein, *Everybody's Autobiography*, p. 138.

26 Stein, *The Making of Americans*, p. 134.

27 Gertrude Stein, *As Fine as Melanctha (1914–1930)*, vol. IV of *The Yale Edition of the Unpublished Writings of Gertrude Stein* (New Haven, CT, 1954), p. 158.

28 Stein, *Selected Writings*, p. 71.

29 Stein, *Everybody's Autobiography*, p. 157.

30 Miller, *Gertrude Stein*, p. 109.

31 Stein, *Everybody's Autobiography*, p. 16; Stein, *Wars I Have Seen*, p. 36.

32 Gertrude Stein, 'In the Red Deeps', in Miller, *Gertrude Stein*, p. 108.

33 Stein, *Everybody's Autobiography*, p. 142.

34 Stein, *Selected Writings*, p. 68.

Two

 1 Alice Toklas said Stein was 'very Californian . . . almost a foreigner' when she went East, quoted in Brenda Wineapple, *Sister Brother: Gertrude and Leo Stein* (London, 1997), p. 45.

 2 Gertrude Stein, college theme, in Rosalind S. Miller, *Gertrude Stein: Form and Intelligibility* (New York, 1949), p. 115.

3 Gertrude Stein, 'In the Library', ibid., p. 141.

4 Ibid., p. 120.

5 Ibid., p. 115.

6 Evidence supporting Stein's sensitivity over charges of literary incompetence is found in her tutor's comments: 'standpoint of a morbid psychological state'; 'awkward and unidiomatic uses of language'; 'wretched sentence structure'; 'incoherent'; 'lacking in organization, in fertility of resource, and in artfulness of literary method', ibid., pp. 108–56.

7 Miller suggests that 'Woman' displays 'an antipathy [Stein] harboured all her life' towards illogical and hysterical women, ibid., p. 103.

8 Gertrude Stein, *Selected Writings of Gertrude Stein* (New York, 1972), p. 78.

9 Brenda Wineapple provides a coherent narrative of Stein's movements and her preoccupations in these years, see *Sister Brother: Gertrude and Leo Stein* (London, 1997).

10 William James quoted by Bert Bender, *The Descent of Love* (Philadelphia, PA, 1996), p. 118. See, for example, Münsterberg, *The Americans* (1905), Santayana, *Character and Opinion in the United States* (1920) and Royce, *Race Questions* (1908).

11 See Steven Meyer, *Irresistible Dictation: Gertrude Stein and the Correlations of Writing and Science* (Stanford, CA, 2001). Meyer provides an exhaustive reading of the relation of Stein's scientific training to her later work.

12 Mina Loy, 'Gertrude Stein', *Transatlantic Review*, II/3 (October 1924).

13 Donald Gallup, ed., *The Flowers of Friendship: Letters Written to Gertrude Stein* (New York, 1953), p. 4.

14 Stein, *Selected Writings*, pp. 74–5.

15 See Tim Armstrong, *Modernism, Technology and the Body: A Cultural Study* (Cambridge, 1998), pp. 197–214.

16 See Wineapple, *Sister Brother*, p. 80.

17 Gertrude Stein and Leon Solomons, 'Normal Motor Automatism', *Motor Automatism* (New York, 1969), p. 10.

18 See Nancy Leys Stepan and Sander L. Gilman, 'Appropriating the Idioms of Science: The Rejection of Scientific Racism', *The Bounds of Race: Perspectives on Hegemony and Resistance*, ed. Dominick LaCapra (Ithaca, NY, 1991), pp. 72–103.

19 Meyer, *Irresistible Dictation*, p. 221.

20 Quoted in *Newsweek*, 8 December 1934, p. 24.

21 Gertrude Stein, 'A Transatlantic Interview 1946', in *A Primer for the Gradual Understanding of Gertrude Stein*, ed. Robert Bartlett Haas (Los Angeles, CA, 1971), p. 18.

22 Gertrude Stein, *Narration: Four Lectures* (Westport, CT, 1969), p. 15.

23 James R. Mellow, *Charmed Circle: Gertrude Stein and Company* (New York, 1974), p. 33.

24 Meyer, *Irresistible Dictation*, p. xvii.

25 Ibid., p. xxi.

26 Gertrude Stein, 'Possessive Case', in *As Fine as Melanctha* (1914–1930), vol. IV of *The Yale Edition of the Unpublished Writings of Gertrude Stein* (New Haven, CT, 1954), p. 144.

27 See Wineapple, *Sister Brother*, p. 81. See also Armstrong, *Modernism, Technology, and the Body*, p. 199, for a discussion of Stein's 'distracted writing'.

28 Quoted in Meyer, *Irresistible Dictation*, p. xv.

29 Gertrude Stein, 'Ocean Symphony', in Miller, *Gertrude Stein*, p. 121.

30 Stein, *Selected Writings*, p. 74.

31 Gertrude Stein, *Lectures in America* (New York, 1975), p. 137.

32 Laura Marcus, *Auto/biographical Discourses: Criticism, Theory, Practice* (Manchester, 1994), p. 67.

33 See Wineapple, *Sister Brother*, pp. 103–4.

34 Gertrude Stein, 'The Value of College Education for Women', in Wineapple, *Sister Brother*, p. 105.

35 Stein, *The Making of Americans* (Normal, IL, 1995), p. 783.

36 Ibid., p. 349.

37 Stein's description for the dust jacket of *Geography and Plays* (Boston, MA, 1922).

38 Meyer, *Irresistible Dictation*, p. 79.

39 Lewellys F. Barker, *The Nervous System and Its Constituent Neurones* (New York, 1899), pp. 725–6.

40 Stein, *The Making of Americans*, p. 375.

41 Lewellys F. Barker, *Time and the Physician* (New York, 1942), p. 60.

42 Bender, *The Descent of Love*, pp. 156ff. Bender concentrates on William Dean Howell's *Dr Breen's Practice* (1881), Elizabeth Stuart Phelps's *Dr Zay* (1882), Sarah Orne Jewett's *A Country Doctor*, and Henry James's

The Bostonians (1886).

43 Wineapple's chronology of the events of Stein's student years, and her self-perception at the time, informs my reading of them here. See *Sister Brother*, pp. 123–31; 140–44; 149–51.

44 Stein, *Selected Writings*, p. 77.

45 See Wineapple, *Sister Brother*, p. 141.

46 Stein, *Selected Writings*, p. 78.

47 Stein, *Everybody's Autobiography* (New York, 1937), p. 264.

48 'Then they make a baby to make for themselves a new beginning and so win for themselves a new everlasting feeling.' Stein, *Lectures in America*, p. 150. See Meyer, *Irresistible Dictation*, p. 210.

49 This essay, probably written between October 1901 and early 1902, was discovered and attributed to Stein by Brenda Wineapple; see Wineapple, *Sister Brother*, pp. 409–14. See also Wineapple's commentary on the essay, pp. 152–4.

50 Of course Stein was not alone in linking the decadent and the New Woman. See Linda Dowling, 'The Decadent and the New Woman in the 1890s', *Nineteenth Century Fiction*, XXXIII/4 (1979), pp. 434–53.

51 Wineapple, *Sister Brother*, p. 123.

52 Ibid., p. 413.

53 Ibid., p. 154.

54 Ibid., p. 181.

55 These recollections are quoted by Meyer, *Irresistible Dictation*, p. 86.

56 Stein, *Selected Writings*, p. 77.

57 Ibid., p. 78.

58 Edmund Wilson, *Upstate: Records and Recollections of Northern New York* (London, 1972), p. 63.

59 Gertrude Stein, *Fernhurst, QED, and Other Early Writings by Gertrude Stein*, ed. Leon Katz (New York, 1971), p. 102.

60 Ibid., p. 58.

61 Ibid., p. 100.

62 Leon Katz, introduction to Stein, *Fernhurst, QED, and Other Early Writings*, p. xviii.

63 Gertrude Stein, 'Why do Americans Live in Europe?', *Transition*, XIV (1928), pp. 97–8.

64 Gertrude Stein, 'The Making of Americans', in *Fernhurst, QED, and Other Early Writings*, p. 153.

Three

1 Robert McAlmon and Kay Boyle, *Being Geniuses Together* (London, 1970), p. 241.
2 Leon Katz was the first to explore Stein's depression, in his doctoral thesis on *The Making of Americans*, 'The First Making of *The Making of Americans*: A Study Based on Gertrude Stein's Notebooks and Early Versions of Her Novel (1902–8)', PhD dissertation, Columbia University (1963). Although unpublished, his thesis has been a fount of information for Stein critics. Some of his points about the affair with May Bookstaver and Stein's state of mind at this time are reiterated in his introduction to QED. See Gertrude Stein, *Fernhurst, QED, and Other Early Writings by Gertrude Stein*, ed. Leon Katz (New York, 1971).
3 Stein, *Fernhurst, QED, and Other Early Writings*, p. 19.
4 Shari Benstock, *Women of the Left Bank: Paris 1900–1940* (London, 1987), p. 178.
5 Stein, *Fernhurst, QED, and Other Early Writings*, p. 80.
6 Benstock, *Women of the Left Bank*, p. 189.
7 James R. Mellow, *Charmed Circle: Gertrude Stein and Company* (New York, 1974), p. 4.
8 Maurice Grosser, 'Maurice Grosser on Gertrude Stein and Alice Toklas', in *The Company They Kept: Writers on Unforgettable Friendships*, ed. Robert B. Silvers and Barbara Epstein (New York, 2006), p. 154.
9 'Removed from [the American] literary heritage, Stein did not suffer an anxiety of influence.' Benstock, *Women of the Left Bank*, p. 192. See also p. 149 on Stein's domestic situation.
10 Ibid., p. 47.
11 Paul Bowles, *Without Stopping: An Autobiography* (London, 1972), p. 119.
12 Brenda Wineapple, *Sister Brother: Gertrude and Leo Stein* (London, 1997), p. 139.
13 Stein, *Fernhurst, QED, and Other Early Writings*, p. 34.
14 Ibid., p. 29.
15 Gertrude Stein, *Selected Writings of Gertrude Stein* (New York, 1972), p. 42.
16 Ibid., p. 117.

17 Ibid., p. 50.

18 John Richardson, *A Life of Picasso* (London, 1996), vol. I, p. 396.

19 Gertrude Stein, *Picasso* (London, 1946), p. 18.

20 Stein, *Selected Writings*, p. 42.

21 See Benstock, *Women of the Left Bank*, p. 153.

22 Stein, *Selected Writings*, p. 47.

23 Janet Hobhouse, *Everybody Who Was Anybody: A Biography of Gertrude Stein* (London, 1975), p. 49.

24 Quoted in Mellow, *Charmed Circle*, p. 97.

25 Mabel Dodge Luhan, *European Experiences* (New York, 1935), p. 324.

26 Stein, *Selected Writings*, p. 66.

27 Ibid., p. 49.

28 Richardson, *A Life of Picasso*, vol. I, p. 455.

29 Stein, *Selected Writings*, p. 12.

30 Stein, *Picasso*, p. 8.

31 Stein, *Selected Writings*, p. 43.

32 Janet Flanner, 'Memory Is All: Alice B. Toklas', in *The Literature of Lesbianism: A Historical Anthology from Ariosto to Stonewall*, ed. Terry Castle (New York, 2003), p. 1073.

33 Richardson, *A Life of Picasso*, vol. I, p. 409.

34 Stein, *Selected Writings*, p. 22.

35 Richardson, *A Life of Picasso*, vol. II, p. 223.

36 Stein, *Selected Writings*, p. 31.

37 Mabel Dodge Luhan reproduced a letter from Stein in which she tells this story in the third volume of her memoirs, *Movers and Shakers* (New York, 1936), p. 33.

38 Edmund Wilson, 'Nonsense', *The New Republic*, 20 February 1929. Reproduced in Kirk Curnutt, ed., *The Critical Response to Gertrude Stein* (Westport, CT, 2000), p. 46.

39 See Richard Bridgman, *Gertrude Stein in Pieces* (New York, 1970), pp. 47–52.

40 Richard Wright, 'Gertrude Stein's Story Is Drenched in Hitler's Horrors', *PM*, 11 March 1945, p. 15.

41 Claude McKay, *A Long Way from Home* (New York, 1970), p. 248.

42 Stein, *Selected Writings*, pp. 63; 46.

43 Quoted in Wineapple, *Sister Brother*, p. 235.

44 Stein, *Fernhurst, QED, and Other Early Writings*, p. 57.

45 There is also the sense of Pound's 'tale of the tribe', the phrase used in *Guide to Kulchur* to describe the *Cantos*.

46 For example, these were terms Robert McAlmon used in a contemporary review of her work, 'The Legend of Gertrude Stein', which appeared in *Outlook* and was reproduced in McAlmon and Boyle, *Being Geniuses Together*, p. 207.

47 Michael North, *The Dialect of Modernism: Race, Language and Twentieth-Century Literature* (New York, 1994), pp. 59–76.

48 See Janice L. Doane, *Silence and Narrative: The Early Novels of Gertrude Stein* (Westport, CT, 1986), p. 138.

49 See Gertrude Stein, 'Lecture II – Narration' [1935], in *The Poetics of the New American Poetry*, ed. Donald Allen and Warren Tallman (New York, 1973), pp. 106–13.

50 Gertrude Stein, *Three Lives* (London, 1990), p. 62.

51 Peter Keating, *The Haunted Study: A Social History of the English Novel, 1875–1914* (London, 1991), p. 234.

52 Donald Gallup, ed., *The Flowers of Friendship: Letters Written to Gertrude Stein* (New York, 1953), p. 47. Galsworthy was an unenthusiastic recipient; Wells, after initial bewilderment, professed to admire the work and made repeated plans to meet up with Stein, but never did. There is no record of what either Bennett or Shaw made of the book.

53 Ibid., p. 50.

54 Stein told Carl Van Vechten that reality, rather than realism, was 'what interests me most in the world', in a letter of 5 October 1929. Edward Burns, ed., *The Letters of Gertrude Stein and Carl Van Vechten, 1913–1946*, vol. I (1913–1935) (New York, 1986), p. 203.

Four

1 Gertrude Stein, autobiographical notes for *Geography and Plays*, 1922, Yale Collection of American Literature.

2 Anonymous, 'Gertrude Stein in Critical French Eyes', *The Literary Digest*, 6 February 1926. Reproduced in Kirk Curnutt, ed., *The Critical Response to Gertrude Stein* (Westport, CT, 2000), p. 32.

3 William Carlos Williams, *Autobiography* (New York, 1951), p. 237.

4 See, for example, Charles W. Chessnut on 'the formation of a future American race', in 'The Future American' (1900), in *Theories of Ethnicity*, ed. Werner Sollors (New York, 1989), p. 17, or Theodore Roosevelt's 1888 study of Governor Morris in *Theodore Roosevelt: An American Mind* (New York, 1994), p. 95.

5 Anonymous review, *Daily Oklahoman*, 25 February 1934.

6 One reviewer compared it to *Buddenbrooks* and *The Forsyte Saga*; anonymous review, *New York Nation*, 11 April 1934.

7 Suzanne Clark's idea of an attempt to 'restore the sentimental *within* modernism, and the sense of great struggle over subjectivity that the resulting contradictions precipitated' is relevant here; see Suzanne Clark, *Sentimental Modernism: Women Writers and the Revolution of the Word* (Bloomington, IN, 1991), p. 4.

8 Gertrude Stein, *The Making of Americans* (Normal, IL, 1995), p. 283.

9 Letter from Gertrude Stein to Rousseau Voorhies, *Chicago Daily News*, 14 March 1934.

10 Stein, *The Making of Americans*, p. 574.

11 Gertrude Stein, 'The Gradual Making of The Making of Americans', in *Selected Writings of Gertrude Stein* (New York, 1972), p. 246.

12 Richard Bridgman, *Gertrude Stein in Pieces* (New York, 1970), p. 73.

13 See Otto Weininger, *Sex and Character* (London, 1906). This is the first English translation, which Stein would have read.

14 For discussion of Stein's reading of Lombroso and Weininger see Ulla Dydo, 'To Have the Winning Language', in *Coming to Light*, ed. Diane Wood Middlebrook and Marilyn Yalom (Ann Arbor, MI, 1985), pp. 58–73.

15 For a varied and informative overview of Weininger criticism, see Nancy A. Harrowitz and Barbara Hyams, eds, *Jews and Gender: Responses to Otto Weininger* (Philadelphia, PA, 1995).

16 See Rosalind Miller, *Gertrude Stein: Form and Intelligibility* (New York, 1949), p. 128.

17 Gertrude Stein, *Painted Lace and Other Pieces: 1914–1937* (New Haven, CT, 1955), p. 94.

18 Maria Damon discusses this extract in 'Gertrude Stein's Jewishness, Jewish Social Scientists, and the "Jewish Question"', *Modern Fiction Studies*, XLII/3 (1996), p. 503.

19 See Linda Wagner-Martin, *'Favored Strangers': Gertrude Stein and Her*

Family (New Brunswick, NJ, 1995), p. 185.

20 Stein, *Selected Writings*, p. 11.

21 Horace Kallen, 'Democracy versus the Melting-Pot' [1915], in *Theories of Ethnicity: A Classical Reader*, ed. Werner Sollors (New York, 1996), p. 91.

22 Stein, *The Making of Americans*, p. 3.

23 Ibid., p. 459.

24 Roland Barthes, *The Pleasure of the Text*, trans. Richard Miller (Oxford, 1990), p. 14.

25 Gertrude Stein, *Narration* (Chicago, IL, 1935), p. 52.

26 Stein, *The Making of Americans*, p. 227. See Jayne L. Walker, 'History as Repetition', in *Modern Critical Views: Gertrude Stein*, ed. Harold Bloom (New York, 1986), p. 178.

27 Stein, *The Making of Americans*, p. 593.

28 Gertrude Stein, 'A Transatlantic Interview 1946', in *A Primer for the Gradual Understanding of Gertrude Stein*, ed. Robert Bartlett Haas (Los Angeles, CA, 1971), p. 20.

29 Stein, *The Making of Americans*, p. 33.

30 Donald Gallup, ed., *The Flowers of Friendship: Letters Written to Gertrude Stein* (New York, 1953). Michael Gold similarly stated that Stein's 'art became a personal pleasure, a private hobby, a vice', in 'Gertrude Stein: A Literary Idiot', *Change the World!* (London, 1937), p. 25.

31 Stein's response is quoted by Brenda Wineapple, *Sister Brother: Gertrude and Leo Stein* (London, 1997), p. 335.

32 Gertrude Stein, Catalogue, Riba-Rovira Exhibition, Galerie Roquepine (Paris, 1945), reproduced in *Pictures for a Picture of Gertrude Stein*, ed. Lamont Moore (New Haven, CT, 1951), p. 18.

33 See Steven Meyer, *Irresistible Dictation: Gertrude Stein and the Correlations of Writing and Science* (Stanford, CA, 2001), p. 295.

34 Gertrude Stein, *Two: Gertrude Stein and Her Brother, and Other Early Portraits* (New Haven, CT, 1951), introduction by Janet Flanner, p. xiii.

35 James R. Mellow, *Charmed Circle: Gertrude Stein and Company* (New York, 1974), p. 181.

36 Gertrude Stein, 'Farragut or A Husband's Recompense', in *Useful Knowledge* (New York, 1929), p. 13.

37 See Lucia Re, 'The Salon and Literary Modernism', in *Jewish Women and their Salons: The Power of Conversation*, ed. Emily D. Bilski and

Emily Braun (New Haven, CT, 2005), p. 190.

38 Mellow, *Charmed Circle*, p. 192.

39 Gertrude Stein, *Geography and Plays* (Boston, MA, 1922), p. 192.

40 See Bilski and Braun, *Jewish Women and their Salons*, p. 237.

Five

1 See Sharon Marcus, *Between Women: Friendship, Desire and Marriage in Victorian England* (Princeton, NJ, 2007), pp. 193–255.

2 Mabel Dodge Luhan, *European Experiences* (New York, 1935), p. 325.

3 See Linda Simon, *The Biography of Alice B. Toklas* (London, 1991).

4 Terry Castle, ed., *The Literature of Lesbianism: A Historical Anthology from Ariosto to Stonewall* (New York, 2003), p. 32.

5 See Shari Benstock, *Women of the Left Bank: Paris 1900–1940* (London, 1987), p. 175.

6 See George Wickes, 'A Natalie Barney Garland', *The Paris Review* (Spring 1975), pp. 115–16.

7 Gertrude Stein, *Selected Writings* (New York, 1972), p. 109.

8 Gertrude Stein, *Fernhurst, QED, and Other Early Writings by Gertrude Stein*, ed. Leon Katz (New York, 1971), p. 118.

9 See Richard Bridgman, *Gertrude Stein in Pieces* (New York, 1970), p. 46.

10 Ibid., p. 119.

11 Gertrude Stein, *Matisse Picasso and Gertrude Stein with Two Shorter Stories* (Paris, 1933), p. 266.

12 'A Transatlantic Interview 1946', in *A Primer for the Gradual Understanding of Gertrude Stein*, ed. Robert Bartlett Haas (Los Angeles, CA, 1973), p. 17.

13 Benstock, *Women of the Left Bank*, p. 157.

14 Neil Schmitz, *Of Huck and Alice: Humorous Writing in American Literature* (Minneapolis, MN, 1983), p. 194. As Schmitz says, it 'splinters' from the 'methodical' prose of *The Making of Americans* to the poetry of *Tender Buttons*.

15 Stein, *Matisse Picasso and Gertrude Stein*, p. 115.

16 Ibid., p. 116.

17 Ibid., p. 17.

18 Ibid., p. 115.

19 Gertrude Stein, *Tender Buttons* (New York, 1914), p. 58.

20 Ibid., p. 70.

21 'New Outbreaks of Futurism: "Tender Buttons," Curious Experiment of Gertrude Stein in Literary Anarchy', in *The Critical Response to Gertrude Stein*, ed. Kirk Curnutt (Westport, CT, 2000), p. 18.

22 Quoted in James R. Mellow, *Charmed Circle: Gertrude Stein and Company* (New York, 1974), p. 258.

23 Stein, *Selected Writings*, pp. 147–8.

24 Brenda Wineapple has drawn attention to this process in Stein's 'Possessive Case', for example. See Wineapple, *Sister Brother: Gertrude and Leo Stein* (London, 1997), p. 387.

25 Gertrude Stein, *Bee Time Vine* (New Haven, CT, 1953), p. 80.

26 Gertrude Stein, *Geography and Plays* (Boston, MA, 1922), p. 302.

27 Cynthia Secor wrote that Stein 'was truly radical in her belief that gender is meaningless'; see Cynthia Secor, 'Gertrude Stein: The Complex Force of Her Femininity', in *Women, the Arts, and the 1920s in Paris and New York*, ed. Kenneth W. Wheeler and Virginia Lee Lussier (New Brunswick, NJ, 1982), pp. 27–35.

28 Stein, *Geography and Plays*, p. 18.

29 Gertrude Stein, 'This is the Dress, Aider', in *Tender Buttons*, p. 29.

30 Stein, *Bee Time Vine*, p. 91.

31 Stein, *Selected Writings*, p. 134.

32 Quoted in Mabel Dodge Luhan, *Movers and Shakers* (New York, 1936), p. 33.

33 Quoted in Mellow, *Charmed Circle*, p. 171.

34 Quoted in Luhan, *Movers and Shakers*, p. 35.

35 Stein, *Selected Writings*, p. 150.

36 Janet Hobhouse, *Everybody Who Was Anybody: A Biography of Gertrude Stein* (London, 1975), p. 110.

37 Quoted in Wineapple, *Sister Brother*, p. 2.

38 The title of a critical piece published by Robert McAlmon in *Outlook* was 'The Legend of Gertrude Stein'.

39 Alice B. Toklas, *What Is Remembered* (London, 1963), p. 127.

Six

1 Gertrude Stein, *Selected Writings of Gertrude Stein* (New York, 1972), p. 84.

2 'Medals for Miss Stein', *New York Tribune*, 13 May 1923, in Kirk Curnutt, ed., *The Critical Response to Gertrude Stein* (Westport, CT, 2000), p. 23.

3 In *The Autobiography of Alice B. Toklas*, Stein mentions proudly that Madame Récamier came from Belley, the region of France where she and Toklas had their country home; Stein, *Selected Writings*, p. 210.

4 See Robert A. Martin and Linda Wagner-Martin, 'The Salons of Wharton's Fiction', in *Wretched Exotic: Essays on Edith Wharton in Europe*, ed. Katherine Joslin and Alan Price (New York, 1993), pp. 105–6; and Shari Benstock, *Women of the Left Bank: Paris 1900–1940* (London, 1987), pp. 34–45.

5 Stein, *Selected Writings*, p. 12.

6 Ibid.

7 Donald Gallup, ed., *The Flowers of Friendship: Letters Written to Gertrude Stein* (New York, 1953), p. 48.

8 Stein, *Selected Writings*, p. 116.

9 Frederick A. Sweet, *Miss Mary Cassatt: Impressionist from Pennsylvania* (Norman, OK, 1966), p. 196.

10 James R. Mellow, *Charmed Circle: Gertrude Stein and Company* (New York, 1974), p. 178.

11 Ibid., p. 180.

12 Quoted in Brenda Wineapple, *Sister Brother: Gertrude and Leo Stein* (London, 1997), p. 397.

13 For a discussion of Jewish salons, see Emily D. Bilski and Emily Braun, eds, *Jewish Women and their Salons: The Power of Conversation* (New Haven, CT, 2005).

14 Stein, *Selected Writings*, p. 46.

15 See Bilski and Braun, *Jewish Women and their Salons*, p. 115.

16 Gertrude Stein, *As Fine as Melanctha* (1914–1930), vol. IV of *The Yale Edition of the Unpublished Writings of Gertrude Stein* (New Haven, CT, 1954), foreword by Natalie Barney, p. xii.

17 Ernest Hemingway, *A Moveable Feast* (London, 1964), p. 18.

18 Robert McAlmon and Kay Boyle, *Being Geniuses Together* (London, 1970), p. 204.

19 Robert Bartlett Haas, *A Primer for the Gradual Understanding of Gertrude Stein* (Los Angeles, CA, 1973), p. 13.

20 For an interesting reading of Stein's orality, see Lucia Re, 'The Salon and Literary Modernism', in *Jewish Women and their Salons*, ed. Bilski and Braun, pp. 188–93.

21 Maurice Grosser, 'Maurice Grosser on Gertrude Stein and Alice Toklas', in *The Company They Kept: Writers on Unforgettable Friendships*, ed. Robert B. Silvers and Barbara Epstein (New York, 2006), p. 154.

22 See Emily D. Bilski and Emily Braun, 'Expatriates and Avant-Gardes', in *Jewish Women and their Salons*, ed. Bilski and Braun, p. 125.

23 Ibid., pp. 10; 117.

24 To appreciate the malicious element to this type of criticism one only need look at Wyndham Lewis's *Time and Western Man*, wherein he described Stein's writing as 'a cold suet-roll of fabulously reptilian length. Cut it at any point, it is the same thing; the same heavy, sticky, opaque mass all through . . . all fat without nerve . . . the life is a low-grade, if tenacious one.' *Time and Western Man* (London, 1927), p. 77.

25 Gertrude Stein, *Everybody's Autobiography* (New York, 1937).

26 Lewis, *Time and Western Man*, p. 78.

27 Sylvia Beach, *Shakespeare and Company* (New York, 1959), p. 29.

28 Stein, *Selected Writings*, p. 203.

29 Quoted in Janet Hobhouse, *Everybody Who Was Anybody: A Biography of Gertrude Stein* (London, 1975), p. 185.

30 See Mellow, *Charmed Circle*, p. 252.

31 Stein, *Selected Writings*, p. 190.

32 Quoted in Simon, *The Biography of Alice B. Toklas*, pp. 157–8.

33 *The Letters of Gertrude Stein and Carl Van Vechten 1913–1946*, ed. Edward Burns, vol. I (1913–1935) (New York, 1986), p. 236.

34 Hemingway, *A Moveable Feast*, p. 30.

35 Alice B. Toklas, *What Is Remembered* (London, 1963), p. 117.

36 Beach, *Shakespeare and Company*, p. 32.

37 Paul Bowles, *Without Stopping* (London, 1972), pp. 120–21.

38 Gertrude Stein, *Wars I Have Seen* (London, 1945), p. 3.

39 Quoted in Simon, *The Biography of Alice B. Toklas*, p. 158.

40 Françoise Gilot and Carlton Lake, *Life with Picasso* (Harmondsworth, 1964), p. 62.

41 Ernest Hemingway, 'The True Story of My Break with Gertrude Stein', in *The Critical Response*, ed. Curnutt, p. 254.

42 See Linda Wagner-Martin, *'Favored Strangers': Gertrude Stein and Her Family* (New Brunswick, NJ, 1995), p. 201.

43 Hemingway, *A Moveable Feast*, p. 22.

44 Stein, *Everybody's Autobiography*, p. 119.

45 See Emily D. Bilski and Emily Braun, 'Expatriates and Avant-Gardes', in *Jewish Women and their Salons*, ed. Bilski and Braun, p. 125: 'Speaking in earnest gave way to the importance of seeing and being seen. Stein helped turn literature into sound bites and salons into show business.'

46 Carl Van Vechten, 'How to Read Gertrude Stein', in *Gertrude Stein Remembered*, ed. Linda Simon (Lincoln, NE, 1994), p. 44.

47 Stein, *Selected Writings*, p. 116.

48 Benstock, *Women of the Left Bank*, p. 47.

49 Benstock draws attention to the different values of Barney's and Stein's salons, ibid., p. 15; p. 86.

50 Beach, *Shakespeare and Company*, p. 31.

51 Bravig Imbs, *Confessions of Another Young Man* (New York, 1936), p. 116.

52 Grosser, 'Maurice Grosser on Gertrude Stein and Alice B. Toklas', p. 159.

53 Richard Bridgman, *Gertrude Stein in Pieces* (New York, 1970), p. 162.

54 Ibid., p. 164.

55 McAlmon and Boyle, *Being Geniuses Together*, p. 228.

56 Michael Gold, *Change the World!* (London, 1937), p. 25.

57 B. L. Reid, *Art by Subtraction* (Norman, OK, 1958), p. 207.

58 Quoted in Curnutt, *The Critical Response*, p. 28.

59 Robert McAlmon managed to use just about all of them in his 'Portrait' of Stein, written in the form of a parody of her writing; he calls her 'a Sumerian monument' possessing a 'jungle-muddy forestial mind naively intellectualizing'; associates her thought processes with 'biblical slime' and 'oracular proclamations . . . mediumistic deliverances'; calls her an 'aged elephant' . . . 'heaving from the slime' . . . 'a slow child' (McAlmon and Boyle, *Being Geniuses Together*, pp. 228–30).

60 Edmund Wilson, *Axel's Castle* (New York, 1931), p. 239; 252.

61 Mellow, *Charmed Circle*, p. 294.

62 Harold Acton, *Memoirs of an Aesthete* (London, 1948), pp. 161–2.

63 Stein, *Selected Writings*, p. 221.

64 Ibid., p. 66.

Seven

1 Gertrude Stein, *The Making of Americans* (Normal, IL, 1995), p. 573.

2 On Stein and Whitman see Joseph Fichtelberg, *The Complex Image: Faith and Method in American Autobiography* (Philadelphia, PA, 1989), pp. 170–71; G. Thomas Couser, 'Of Time and Identity: Walt Whitman and Gertrude Stein as Autobiographers', *Texas Studies in Literature and Language*, XVII/4 (1976), pp. 787–804.

3 Quoted in Janet Hobhouse, *Everybody Who Was Anybody: A Biography of Gertrude Stein* (London, 1975), p. 157.

4 Gertrude Stein, *How to Write* (Los Angeles, CA, 1995), p. 420.

5 Quoted in Hobhouse, *Everybody Who Was Anybody*, p. 141.

6 Gertrude Stein, *Selected Writings* (New York, 1972), p. vii.

7 See Hobhouse, *Everybody Who Was Anybody*, p. 142.

8 Gertrude Stein, *Everybody's Autobiography* (New York, 1937), p. 50.

9 Stein, *Selected Writings*, pp. 118; 222.

10 Stein's role in the American humorous tradition was imaginatively expounded by Neil Schmitz, *Of Huck and Alice: Humorous Writing in American Literature* (Minneapolis, MN, 1983).

11 Janet Flanner, introduction to Gertrude Stein, *Two: Gertrude Stein and Her Brother, and Other Early Portraits* (New Haven, CT, 1951), p. ix.

12 This is a point recently made by Noel Sloboda in his work on the autobiographies of Stein and Edith Wharton, a fascinating and fruitful comparison if only for their many divergences. See Noel Sloboda, *The Making of Americans in Paris: The Autobiographies of Edith Wharton and Gertrude Stein* (New York, 2008).

13 Stein, *Selected Writings*, p. 17.

14 Catharine R. Stimpson, 'Gertrude Stein and the Lesbian Lie', in Margo Culley, ed., *American Women's Autobiography: Fea(s)ts of Memory* (Madison, WI, 1992), pp. 156; 161.

15 Ibid., p. 153.

16 Ibid., p. 153.

17 Stein, *Selected Writings*, p. 189.

18 Ibid., pp. 203–4.

19 Hapgood to Hemingway, 27 May 1937, quoted in Hutchins Hapgood, *A Victorian in the Modern World* (New York, 1939), p. 535. Hapgood remembers how Stein 'talked to me for a long time about how impossible it was for a Jewish woman to marry a Gentile', remarking on what he saw as Stein's intense Jewishness.

20 Quoted in Linda Simon, *The Biography of Alice B. Toklas* (London, 1991), p. 152.

21 Quoted in Hobhouse, *Everybody Who Was Anybody*, p. 167.

22 James R. Mellow, *Charmed Circle: Gertrude Stein and Company* (New York, 1974), p. 356.

23 Donald Sutherland, 'The Pleasures of Gertrude Stein', *The New York Review of Books*, xxi/9 (30 May 1974), pp. 28–9.

24 Georges Braque, Eugene Jolas, Maria Jolas, Henri Matisse, André Salmon, Tristan Tzara, *Testimony Against Gertrude Stein* (The Hague, 1935), p. 2.

25 Stein, *Everybody's Autobiography*, p. 68.

26 Stein, *Selected Writings*, p. 83.

27 Stein, *Everybody's Autobiography*, p. 116.

28 Schmitz, *Of Huck and Alice*, p. 204.

29 See Mellow, *Charmed Circle*, p. 371.

30 'I lost my personality', she said in 'And Now' [1934], in *How Writing Is Written*, vol. ii of the *Previously Uncollected Writings of Gertrude Stein* (Los Angeles, CA, 1974), p. 63.

31 Flanner, introduction to Stein, *Two*, p. xvi.

32 Gertrude Stein, 'A Transatlantic Interview', in *A Primer for the Gradual Understanding of Gertrude Stein*, ed. Robert Bartlett Haas (Los Angeles, CA, 1971), p. 19.

33 Ibid., p. xvii.

34 Hobhouse, *Everybody Who Was Anybody*, p. 163.

35 See Richard Bridgman, *Gertrude Stein in Pieces* (New York, 1970), pp. 213–17.

36 Gertrude Stein, *Stanzas in Meditation* (New Haven, CT, 1956), p. 92.

37 Ibid., p. 283.

38 Stein, *Everybody's Autobiography*, p. 68.

39 Stimpson discusses this doubleness in 'Gertrude Stein and the

Lesbian Lie', p. 152. As Stimpson notes, it depends on the predisposition of the reader which of these Steins is seen as the 'good' Stein and which is seen as the 'bad' Stein.

40 Mellow, *Charmed Circle*, p. 369.
41 Linda Wagner-Martin, *'Favored Strangers': Gertrude Stein and Her Family* (New Brunswick, NJ, 1995), p. 209.
42 Alice B. Toklas, *What is Remembered* (London, 1989), p. 154.
43 Quoted in Wagner-Martin, *'Favored Strangers'*, p. 209.
44 Mellow, *Charmed Circle*, p. 407.
45 Bennett Cerf, *At Random* (New York, 1977), p. 103.
46 Ibid, p. 102.
47 Stein, *Everybody's Autobiography*, p. 129.
48 Kirk Curnutt, ed., *The Critical Response to Gertrude Stein* (Westport, CT, 2000), p. 4.
49 Richard Bridgman, *Gertrude Stein in Pieces* (New York, 1970), p. 14.
50 Schmitz, *Of Huck and Alice*, p. 224.
51 Quoted in Simon, *The Biography of Alice B. Toklas*, p. 202.
52 Gertrude Stein, *Lectures in America* (New York, 1935), p. 34.
53 Ibid., p. 203.
54 Thornton Wilder, introduction to Gertrude Stein, *Four in America* (New Haven, CT, 1947), p. vi.
55 Cerf, *At Random*, p. 102.
56 Isaac Goldberg, 'A Stein on the Table', *Panorama*, April 1934.
57 Curnutt, *The Critical Response to Gertrude Stein*.
58 Toklas, *What Is Remembered*, p. 161.
59 Stein, *Everybody's Autobiography*, p. 3.
60 Ibid., p. 115.
61 Bridgman, *Gertrude Stein in Pieces*, p. 287.
62 Stein, *Lectures in America*, pp. 215; 220.
63 Stein, *Selected Writings*, pp. 198–9.
64 Bridgman, *Gertrude Stein in Pieces*, p. 245.
65 Gertrude Stein, *The Geographical History of America* (Baltimore, MD, 1995), p. 235.

Eight

1 Gertrude Stein, 'The Winner Loses', in *Selected Writings of Gertrude Stein* (New York, 1972), p. 623.

2 James R. Mellow, *Charmed Circle: Gertrude Stein and Company* (New York, 1974), p. 440.

3 Stein, *Selected Writings*, p. 637.

4 Mellow, *Charmed Circle*, p. 451.

5 Alice B. Toklas, *The Alice B. Toklas Cookbook* (New York, 1960), p. 227.

6 Gertrude Stein, *Wars I Have Seen* (London, 1945), pp. 31–2.

7 Ibid., p. 32.

8 Mellow, *Charmed Circle*, p. 456.

9 See Edward Burns and Ulla E. Dydo, Appendix IX: 'Gertrude Stein: September 1942 to September 1944', in *The Letters of Gertrude Stein and Thornton Wilder*, ed. Edward Burns and Ulla E. Dydo (New Haven, CT, 1996), pp. 401–21.

10 Janet Malcolm, *Two Lives: Gertrude and Alice* (New Haven, CT, 2007), p. 99.

11 Stein, *Wars I Have Seen*, p.56.

12 Malcolm, *Two Lives*, p. 52.

13 Stein, *Wars I Have Seen*, p. 32.

14 Quoted in Mellow, *Charmed Circle*, p. 456.

15 Cecil Beaton, *Photobiography* (London, 1951), p. 122.

16 Quoted in Richard Bridgman, *Gertrude Stein in Pieces* (New York, 1970), p. 335.

17 Maria Damon defends Stein from these charges, in a subtle contextualizing essay on Stein's attitude to Judaism, 'Gertrude Stein's Jewishness, Jewish Social Scientists, and the "Jewish Question"', *Modern Fiction Studies*, XLII/3 (1996), pp. 489–506.

18 Gertrude Stein, *Paris France* (London, 1995), p. 38.

19 Burns and Dydo, 'Gertrude Stein', p. 417.

20 See Linda Wagner-Martin, *'Favored Strangers': Gertrude Stein and Her Family* (New Brunswick, NJ, 1995), p. 251.

21 Gertrude Stein, *Mrs Reynolds and Five Earlier Novelettes* (New Haven, CT, 1953), p. 267.

22 Stein, *Wars I Have Seen*, p. 161

23 Janet Hobhouse, *Everybody Who Was Anybody: A Biography of Gertrude*

Stein (London, 1975), p. 226.

24 Beaton, *Photobiography*, p. 122.

25 Bennett Cerf, *At Random* (New York, 1977), pp. 107–8.

26 Gertrude Stein, *Brewsie and Willie* (London, 1988), pp. 82–3.

27 Ibid., pp. 113–4.

28 Gertrude Stein, 'The New Hope in Our "Sad Young Men"', in *How Writing Is Written*, vol. II of the *Previously Uncollected Writings of Gertrude Stein* (Los Angeles, 1974), p. 145.

29 Alice B. Toklas, *What Is Remembered* (London, 1963), p. 186.

30 Janet Flanner, introduction to Gertrude Stein, *Two: Gertrude Stein and Her Brother, and Other Early Portraits* (New Haven, CT, 1951), p. x.

31 *Time*, 15 November 1934, quoted in Richard Bridgman, *Gertrude Stein in Pieces*, p. 340.

32 Quoted in Linda Simon, *The Biography of Alice B. Toklas* (London, 1991), p. 210.

33 Catharine R. Stimpson, 'Humanism and its Freaks', *Boundary 2*, XII/3 (1984), p. 304.

34 Edmund Wilson, *Axel's Castle* (New York, 1931), p. 253.

35 Quoted in Wagner-Martin, *'Favored Strangers'*, p. 261.

36 Hobhouse, *Everybody Who Was Anybody*, p. 93.

37 Catharine R. Stimpson summarized Stein's posthumous reputation (as it stood in 1984) in 'Humanism and Its Freaks'.

38 Gertrude Stein, *The Geographical History of America* (Baltimore, MD, 1995), p. 210.

39 Quoted in Mellow, *Charmed Circle*, p. 371.

40 Stein, *Selected Writings*, p. 203.

41 Shari Benstock, *Women of the Left Bank: Paris 1900–1940* (London, 1987), p. 161.

42 Flanner, introduction to Gertrude Stein, *Two*, p. xvii.

43 Gertrude Stein, *Paris France: Personal Recollections* (London, 1940), p. 21.

44 Gertrude Stein, *Matisse Picasso and Gertrude Stein* (Paris, 1933), p. 13.

45 Gertrude Stein, *Useful Knowledge* (New York, 1929), p. 111.

Select Bibliography

Works by Stein

Three Lives (New York, 1909)
Tender Buttons (New York, 1914)
Geography and Plays (Boston, 1922)
The Making of Americans (Paris, 1925)
Composition as Explanation (London, 1926)
Useful Knowledge (New York, 1928)
Lucy Church Amiably (Paris, 1930)
Before the Flowers of Friendship Faded (Paris, 1931)
How to Write (Paris, 1931)
Operas and Plays (Paris, 1932)
Matisse Picasso and Gertrude Stein with Two Shorter Stories (Paris, 1933)
The Autobiography of Alice B. Toklas (New York, 1933)
Four Saints in Three Acts (New York, 1934)
Portraits and Prayers (New York, 1934)
Lectures in America (New York, 1935)
Narration (Chicago, IL, 1935)
The Geographical History of America (New York, 1936)
Everybody's Autobiography (New York, 1937)
Picasso (London, 1938)
The World Is Round (New York, 1939)
Paris France (London, 1938)
What Are Masterpieces (Los Angeles, CA, 1940)
Ida a Novel (New York, 1941)
Wars I Have Seen (New York, 1945)
Brewsie and Willie (New York, 1946)

Selected Writings of Gertrude Stein, edited with an introduction and notes by Carl Van Vechten (New York, 1946)

In Savoy or Yes Is for a Very Young Man (London, 1946)

Four in America (New Haven, CT, 1947)

Blood on the Dining Room Floor (Pawlet, VT, 1948)

Last Operas and Plays (New York, 1949)

Two (Gertrude Stein and Her Brother) and Other Early Portraits (1908–1912), vol. I of *Yale Edition of the Unpublished Writings of Gertrude Stein* (New Haven, CT, 1951)

Mrs Reynolds and Five Earlier Novelettes (1931–1942), vol. II of *Yale Edition of the Unpublished Writings of Gertrude Stein* (New Haven, CT, 1952)

Bee Time Vine and Other Pieces (1913–1927), vol. III of *Yale Edition of the Unpublished Writings of Gertrude Stein* (New Haven, CT, 1953)

As Fine as Melanctha (1914–1930), vol. IV of *Yale Edition of the Unpublished Writings of Gertrude Stein* (New Haven, CT, 1954)

Painted Lace and Other Pieces (1914–1937), vol. V of *Yale Edition of the Unpublished Writings of Gertrude Stein* (New Haven, CT, 1955)

Stanzas in Meditation and Other Poems (1929–1933), vol. VI of *Yale Edition of the Unpublished Writings of Gertrude Stein* (New Haven, CT, 1956)

Alphabets and Birthdays, vol. VII of *Yale Edition of the Unpublished Writings of Gertrude Stein* (New Haven, CT, 1957)

A Novel of Thank You, vol. VIII of *Yale Edition of the Unpublished Writings of Gertrude Stein* (New Haven, CT, 1958)

Fernhurst, QED, and Other Early Writings by Gertrude Stein, ed. Leon Katz (New York, 1971)

Look At Me Now and Here I Am: Writings and Lectures 1909–45, ed. Patricia Meyerowitz (New York, 1971)

A Primer for the Gradual Understanding of Gertrude Stein, ed. Robert Bartlett Haas (Los Angeles, CA, 1971)

Reflections on the Atomic Bomb, vol. I of the *Previously Uncollected Writings of Gertrude Stein* (Los Angeles, CA, 1973)

How Writing Is Written, vol. II of the *Previously Uncollected Writings of Gertrude Stein*, ed. Robert Bartlett Haas (Los Angeles, CA, 1974)

A Stein Reader, ed. Ulla E. Dydo (Evanston, IL, 1993)

Works about Stein

Armstrong, Tim, *Modernism, Technology and the Body: A Cultural Study*
    (Cambridge, 1998)
Bay-Cheng, Sarah, *Mama Dada: Gertrude Stein's Avant-Garde Theater*
    (New York, 2004)
Berry, Ellen E., *Curved Thought and Textual Wandering: Gertrude Stein's
    Postmodernism* (Ann Arbor, MI, 1992)
Bloom, Harold, ed., *Modern Critical Views: Gertrude Stein* (New York, 1986)
Bowers, Jane Palatini, *'They Watch Me as They Watch This': Gertrude Stein's
    Metadrama* (Philadelphia, PA, 1991)
Bridgman, Richard, *Gertrude Stein in Pieces* (New York, 1970)
Brinnin, John Malcolm, *The Third Rose: Gertrude Stein and her World*
    (Boston, MA, 1959)
Burns, Edward, ed., 'Gertrude Stein Issue', *Twentieth Century Literature*,
    XXIV/1 (Spring 1978)
Caramello, Charles, *Henry James, Gertrude Stein, and the Biographical Act*
    (Chapel Hill, NC, 1996)
Chessman, Harriet Scott, *The Public Is Invited to Dance: Representation, the
    Body, and Dialogue in Gertrude Stein* (Stanford, CA, 1989)
Curnutt, Kirk, ed., *The Critical Response to Gertrude Stein* (Westport, CT,
    2000)
Damon, Maria, *The Dark End of the Street: Margins in American Vanguard
    Poetry* (Minneapolis, MN, 1993)
—, 'Gertrude Stein's Jewishness, Jewish Social Scientists, and the "Jewish
    Question"', *Modern Fiction Studies*, XLII/3 (Fall 1996), pp. 489–506
Dearborn, Mary V., 'Gertrude Stein's *The Making of Americans* as an Ethnic
    Text', in *Pocahontas's Daughters: Gender and Ethnicity in American
    Culture* (New York, 1986), pp. 159–93
Dekoven, Marianne, *A Different Language: Gertrude Stein's Experimental
    Writing* (Madison, WI, 1983)
Doane, Janice, *Silence and Narrative: The Early Novels of Gertrude Stein*
    (Westport, CT, 1986)
Dydo, Ulla E., with William Rice, *The Language that Rises 1923–1934*
    (Evanston, IL, 2003)
Fifer, Elizabeth, *Rescued Readings: A Reconstruction of Gertrude Stein's
    Difficult Texts* (Detroit, MI, 1992)

Giroud, Vincent, *Picasso and Gertrude Stein* (New Haven, CT, 2006)

Hejinian, Lyn, 'Two Stein Talks', 'Three Lives' and 'A Common Sense', in *The Language of Inquiry* (Berkeley, CA, 2000)

Hobhouse, Janet, *Everybody Who Was Anybody: A Biography of Gertrude Stein* (New York, 1975)

Hoffman, Michael J., ed., *Critical Essays on Gertrude Stein* (Boston, MA, 1986)

—, *The Development of Abstractionism in the Writings of Gertrude Stein* (Philadelphia, PA, 1965)

—, ed., *Gertrude Stein* (Boston, MA, 1976)

Katz, Leon, 'The First Making of The Making of Americans: A Study Based on Gertrude Stein's Notebooks and Early Versions of her Novel (1902–8)', PhD dissertation, Columbia University (1963)

Kellner, Bruce, ed., *A Gertrude Stein Companion: Content with the Example* (New York, 1988)

Kostelanetz, Richard, *Gertrude Stein Advanced: An Anthology of Criticism* (Jefferson, NC, 1990)

Malcolm, Janet, *Two Lives: Gertrude and Alice* (New Haven, CT, 2007)

Mellow, James R., *Charmed Circle: Gertrude Stein and Company* (New York, 1974)

Meyer, Steven, *Irresistible Dictation: Gertrude Stein and the Correlations of Writing and Science* (Stanford, CA, 2001)

Miller, Rosalind S., *Gertrude Stein: Form and Intelligibility* (New York, 1949); contains Stein's college themes.

Museum of Modern Art, *Four Americans in Paris: The Collections of Gertrude Stein and her Family*, exh. cat., Museum of Modern Art, New York (New York, 1970)

Neuman, Shirley, *Gertrude Stein: Autobiography and the Problem of Narration* (Victoria, BC, 1979)

—, and Ira B. Nadel, eds, *Gertrude Stein and the Making of Literature* (London, 1988)

North, Michael, *The Dialect of Modernism: Race, Language, and Twentieth-century Literature* (New York, 1994)

Perelman, Bob, *The Trouble with Genius: Reading Pound, Joyce, Stein and Zukofsky* (Berkeley, CA, 1994)

Perloff, Marjorie, *The Poetics of Indeterminacy: Rimbaud to Cage* (Princeton, NJ, 1981)

Ryan, Betsy Alayne, *Gertrude Stein's Theatre of the Absolute* (Ann Arbor, MI, 1984)

Schmitz, Neil, *Of Huck and Alice: Humorous Writing in American Literature* (Minneapolis, MN, 1983)

Simon, Linda, *The Biography of Alice B. Toklas* (New York, 1977)

Steiner, Wendy, *Exact Resemblance to Exact Resemblance: The Literary Portraiture of Gertrude Stein* (New Haven, CT, 1978)

Stimpson, Catharine R., 'Gertrude Stein and the Lesbian Lie', in *American Women's Autobiography: Fea(s)ts of Memory*, ed. Margo Culley (Madison, WI, 1992), pp. 152–66

—, 'Gertrude Stein and the Transposition of Gender', in *The Poetics of Gender*, ed. Nancy K. Miller (New York, 1986), pp. 1–18

—, 'Humanism and Its Freaks', *Boundary 2*, XIII (1984), pp. 301–19

—, 'The Mind, the Body and Gertrude Stein', *Critical Inquiry*, III/3 (1977), pp. 489–506

Toklas, Alice B., *The Alice B. Toklas Cookbook* (New York, 1954)

—, *What Is Remembered* (New York, 1963)

Wagner-Martin, Linda, *'Favored Strangers': Gertrude Stein and Her Family* (New Brunswick, NJ, 1995)

Wald, Priscilla, '"A Losing Self-Sense": *The Making of Americans* and the Anxiety of Identity', in *Constituting Americans: Cultural Anxiety and Narrative Form* (Durham, NC, 1995), pp. 237–98

Walker, Jayne L., *The Making of a Modernist: Gertrude Stein from Three Lives to Tender Buttons* (Amherst, MA, 1984)

Watson, Steven, *Prepare for Saints: Gertrude Stein, Virgil Thomson, and the Mainstreaming of American Modernism* (New York, 1998)

Weinstein, Norman, *Gertrude Stein and the Literature of the Modern Consciousness* (New York, 1970)

Weiss, Lynn M., *Gertrude Stein and Richard Wright: The Poetics and Politics of Modernism* (Jackson, MS, 1998)

White, Ray Lewis, *Gertrude Stein and Alice B. Toklas: A Reference Guide* (Boston, MA, 1984)

Wineapple, Brenda, *Sister Brother: Gertrude and Leo Stein* (New York, 1996)

Internet

<small>PENN</small>sound: Center for Programs in Contemporary Writing at the
University of Pennsylvania.
http://writing.upenn.edu/pennsound/x/Stein.html

Link to recordings of Stein reading from *The Making of Americans*, *Matisse*,
A Valentine to Sherwood Anderson, *If I Told Him: A Completed Portrait of
Picasso*, *The Fifteenth of November . . . T S. Eliot*, *Portrait of Christian
Bérard*, *Madame Recamier. An Opera*, and *How She Bowed to Her
Brother*, plus a 1934 interview with Stein. Working notes by Ulla Dydo.

Letters

Burns, Edward, ed., *The Letters of Gertrude Stein and Carl Van Vechten*.
2 vols: 1913–1935 and 1935–1946 (New York, 1986)
—, ed., *Staying On Alone: Letters of Alice B. Toklas* (New York, 1973)
—, and Ulla E. Dydo, eds, *The Letters of Gertrude Stein and Thornton Wilder*
(New Haven, CT, 1996)
Everett, Patricia R., ed., *A History of Having a Great Many Times Not
Continued to Be Friends: The Correspondence between Mabel Dodge and
Gertrude Stein, 1911–1934* (Albuquerque, NM, 1996)
Gallup, Donald, ed., *The Flowers of Friendship: Letters Written to Gertrude
Stein* (New York, 1953)
Page, Tim, and Vanessa Weeks Page, *Selected Letters of Virgil Thomson*
(New York, 1988)
Steward, Samuel M., ed., *Dear Sammy: Letters from Gertrude Stein and Alice
B. Toklas* (Boston, MA, 1977)
Turner, Kay, ed., *Baby Precious Always Shines: Selected Love Notes between
Gertrude Stein and Alice B. Toklas* (New York, 1999)

Acknowledgements

'Gertrude Stein' by Mina Loy is reprinted courtesy of Roger L. Conover, Mina Loy's editor and literary executor. Extract from Gertrude Stein's autobiographical notes for *Geography and Plays*, the Gertrude Stein and Alice B. Toklas Papers, Yale Collection of American Literature, Beinecke Rare Book and Manuscript Library, reprinted by permission of David Higham Associates, and by kind permission of the Estate of Gertrude Stein through its Literary Executor, Mr Stanford Gann, Jr, of Levin & Gann, PA.

I would like to thank the British Academy for financial support in the making of this book. Thanks also to Kasia Boddy, Ros Coward, Ann Fraser, Rowland Hughes, Cathryn Stone and Paul Vlitos, and thank you above all to Terry Daniel and Annette Daniel, and to José Enrique Martinez Yabar.

Photo Acknowledgements

Photos courtesy of Yale Collection of American Literature, Beinecke Rare Book and Manuscript Library: pp. 6, 10 (© DACS 2009), 15, 26, 33, 51, 67, 79, 96 (© Man Ray Trust/ADAGP, Paris and DACS, London 2009), 101, 115, 123, 129 (© Man Ray Trust/ADAGP, Paris and DACS, London 2009), 130 (© ADAGP, Paris and DACS, London 2009), 135, 157 (© Man Ray Trust/ADAGP, Paris and DACS, London 2009), 160, 162 (by permission of The Carl Van Vechten Trust), 164, 165, 170, 175, 182, 185, 190, 191; photo The Metropolitan Museum of Art, Bequest of Gertrude Stein, 1946 (47.106): p. 65 (Image © The Metropolitan Museum of Art, © Succession Picasso/DACS 2009); photos The Baltimore Museum of Art: The Cone Collection, formed by Dr Claribel Cone and Miss Etta Cone of Baltimore, Maryland: pp. 90 (BMA 1950.300), 128 (BMA 1950.315, © ADAGP, Paris and DACS, London 2009); photo Smithsonian American Art Museum: p. 188 (gift of Mr and Mrs Jacob Kainen and museum purchase through a grant from the National Endowment for the Arts, © ARS, NY AND DACS, London 2009).